Hirzel's Handbook:

How to Operate a Michigan Condo or HOA
(2nd Edition)

Disclaimer

Hirzel Law, PLC has created Hirzel's Handbook to serve as a resource guide for community association board members and property managers to help them successfully operate their associations and avoid basic mistakes; however, please keep in mind that relying on this handbook does not form an attorney–client relationship between Hirzel Law, PLC and the reader. This handbook is to be used for informational purposes only. An experienced community association attorney should be consulted regarding specific questions because the answer to many legal questions can be highly fact-specific and changes in the law may occur after this book is published. If you have specific questions, you can contact Hirzel Law, PLC at hirzellaw.com.

Kevin Hirzel

Table of Contents

--- ⚓ ---

CHAPTER 3: TRANSITIONING THE ASSOCIATION FROM DEVELOPER CONTROL TO OWNER CONTROL 55

Introduction

So, you have volunteered to serve on the board of directors for your condominium or homeowners association—what do you do now? Many people volunteer to serve on a board because they are interested in increasing the property values in their community, accomplishing a major improvement project, solving problems among neighbors, or addressing concerns about the financial health of their association. On the other hand, other people are often thrust into the role of a director simply because nobody else wishes to volunteer and they raised their hand at an association meeting. No matter how you ended up on a board, I can attest firsthand that volunteer service on a community association board is often a thankless job. Similarly, most lawsuits that I am involved in do not arise from bad intentions, but rather from lack of education on the part of the board, lack of education on the part of the owners, failure to have appropriate processes in place, or from having poorly drafted governing documents. The good news is that all these things are easily preventable, and this book will teach you how to avoid many common pitfalls of operating a community association!

One of the biggest traps that a board can fall into is to operate their community association on an informal basis, such as a social club. While fostering a sense of community is important, operating solely on a "neighborly" basis can expose the association, along with its officers and directors, to potential liability. Community associations are complex because the directors and officers that operate nonprofit corporations have fiduciary duties to act in the best interest of the corporation, which often means that difficult decisions must be made. Similarly, community associations are often entrusted with a role similar to that of a municipal government and charged with providing services or policing their communities to ensure that the association's governing documents are followed.

Despite the complexity associated with operating a condominium or homeowners association, most board members do not receive any prior training for these positions. In the community association world, board members are often given the keys to the proverbial car before they are required to take driver's training. Thus, irrespective of whether you are taking control over from the developer in a new condominium project or you have been elected to the board of a seasoned community, you probably need some additional information to learn how to operate the car that is your community association. You will find the answers to all your questions in this book, which will help you understand the following:

- The different types of community associations.

- The basic requirements of operating a condominium or homeowners association.

- The process for transitioning from developer to owner control.

- How to enforce the governing documents.

- How to collect delinquent assessments.

- Signs that your governing documents may need to be updated.

- Common pitfalls associated with the Fair Housing Act.

Finally, before we get started, the last question you may be asking yourself is why should I be listening to this guy? I have an extensive list of accolades and awards that you can view on my website at hirzellaw.com. While these are all things that I am proud of and represent my accomplishments as an attorney, the key to my success has been an infinite thirst for knowledge and focus on providing great customer service. Accordingly, this book is not filled with doomsday scenarios, war stories, sales pitches, or anything of the like. Rather, my goal is to provide you with a straightforward handbook, which is not chock-full of legalese, in which you can easily find answers to the common questions that board members ask me on a daily basis. Some issues will be simple enough to handle on your own, but it is important to know when to ask for help.

My law firm has devoted its entire practice to condominium and homeowners association law and real estate law. I have an unmatched passion for helping community associations that has allowed my law firm to rapidly expand throughout the Midwest. A large portion of our practice is devoted to educating board members and property managers because an ounce of prevention is worth a pound of cure. Accordingly, I hope this book helps you avoid common mistakes so your community association does not have to learn lessons the hard way!

Basic Principles That Govern Community Associations

In Michigan, a community association, be it a condominium association, cooperative, homeowners association, or summer resort association, is defined by a few basic characteristics:

- First, a community association is an organization that can be either incorporated or unincorporated and is responsible for managing and maintaining real property. While unincorporated community associations can legally exist, almost all community associations are organized as nonprofit corporations.

- Second, a community association is composed of members, and in almost all cases, the members must have some form of ownership interest in the real property that is governed by the community association. In most cases, the governing documents make membership mandatory, but some community associations are composed of voluntary members only.

- Third, community associations are governed by contractual agreements between the developer, the community association, and its members. In most cases, the contractual agreements impose restrictions on how the members may use real property and provide a framework for governing the community association. A community association's primary responsibility is to enforce the restrictions and abide by the procedures in the governing documents to preserve property values and protect the health, safety, and welfare of the membership.

- Fourth, community associations almost always involve a financial component, in which the members have an obligation to contribute financially toward the management and maintenance of the real property governed by the community association. In most cases, a community association has the right to secure payment by placing and foreclosing liens if a member does not satisfy their financial obligations.

- Fifth, almost all community associations are governed by at least one statutory scheme, either under federal, state, or municipal law, and in many cases are governed by several different statutory schemes.

Now that you know the basic concepts, we will delve a little bit deeper into the specific types of community associations that exist in Michigan.

Hierarchy of Laws That Apply to Community Associations

When operating a community association, it is important to understand that community associations are subject to federal law, state law, and local ordinances, as well as various governing documents. Generally speaking, the following hierarchy will apply:

- **Federal Law**. Article VI of the United States Constitution contains what is known as the "Supremacy Clause" and states that "This Constitution, and the Laws of the United States which shall be made in Pursuance thereof...shall be the supreme Law of the Land; and the Judges in every State shall be bound thereby, any Thing in the Constitution or Laws of any State to the Contrary notwithstanding." Accordingly, federal statutes, such as the Federal Fair Housing Act, Freedom to Display the American Flag Act, Over-The-Air Reception Device Rules ("OTARD"), and the United States Bankruptcy Code, will take precedence over state law, municipal law, the governing documents, and the Association's rules and regulations.

- **State Law**. Condominiums, platted subdivisions, and community associations are formed under state statutes, such as the Michigan Condominium Act, Michigan Nonprofit Corporation Act, Michigan Land Division Act, and Michigan Summer Resort Act. Accordingly, governing documents should not conflict with these state laws. As recently noted by the Michigan Court of Appeals, "Condominiums are *not* products of common law; they are creatures of statute, and the Legislature gave developers any so called 'contractual rights' via the Act...the Act controls and determines the extent of the Master Deed and amendments." Lakeside Estates Condo Prop Owners Ass'n v Sugar Springs

Dev Co, unpublished per curiam opinion of the Court of Appeals, issued Sept 16, 2021 (Docket No. 354451), p 4.

- **Municipal Law**. Municipalities may adopt local ordinances so long as the ordinances do not conflict with the Michigan Constitution and state statutes or so long as they do not attempt to create another regulatory scheme for a field of law that is covered by a state statute. See, e.g., _Rental Prop Owners Ass'n of Kent Co v Grand Rapids_, 455 Mich 246, 256-57; 566 NW2d 514 (1997). By way of example, municipalities often regulate construction activities, dangerous animals, noise, and property use and restrict rentals under zoning laws. In most cases, the local ordinance will work in conjunction with the governing documents for a community association. If a property owner applied to build a new home in a community, the owner may need approval from both the municipality and the community association. Simply obtaining approval from the municipality would not suffice if the governing documents also required the community association to approve the design and plans.

- **Governing Documents**. As indicated above, governing documents, such as articles of incorporation, bylaws, master deeds, declarations, or restrictive covenants are generally created under some type of state statute. Accordingly, as long as the documents do not conflict with legal requirements imposed by a state or federal statute, they will likely control; however, governing documents cannot change more stringent requirements in local ordinances. By way of example, if the governing documents permitted commercial use of a property in a resident's home but the zoning ordinance prohibited commercial use, the zoning ordinance would control.

- **Rules and Regulations**. In Michigan, most community association boards have authority to enact rules and regulations. Generally speaking, "a rule or regulation is 'a tool to implement or manage existing structural law'...." Meadow Bridge Condo Ass'n v Bosca, 187 Mich App 280, 282; 466 NW2d 303 (1990). Accordingly, rules and regulations cannot be created that alter the governing documents, and the governing documents would control if there was a conflict with the rules and regulations.

Chapter 1

Types of Community Associations

Different Types of Condominium Projects

In Michigan, condominiums are governed by the <u>Michigan Condominium Act, MCL 559.101, et seq.</u> A condominium project is created when a developer records a master deed and condominium bylaws in the Register of Deeds in the county where the condominium is located. The condominium project must be governed by a condominium association, which in most cases is a nonprofit corporation, that is also subject to the master deed and condominium bylaws.

There are five basic types of condominium projects:

- Traditional attached residential condominium projects.

- Detached residential condominium projects (also referred to as "site condominiums").

- Business condominium projects.

- Mixed-use condominium projects.

- Other types of condominium projects.

Traditional Attached Residential Condominium Projects

Traditional attached residential condominium projects are comprised of condominium units and common elements. The owner of a condominium unit is called a "co-owner" because the co-owner jointly owns all the common elements with the other owners; however, each co-owner individually owns their own condominium unit.

A co-owner is typically responsible for maintaining and insuring their unit, which usually encompasses everything contained within the airspace of a unit, including the paint on the walls and floor coverings. A condominium association is usually responsible for maintaining general common elements, usually from the drywall out; however, the condominium documents ultimately control when determining maintenance and insurance responsibilities, which may vary between condominium associations. The condominium documents may also assign limited common elements to a particular unit that a co-owner is responsible for maintaining and insuring. Accordingly, a condominium's master deed and condominium bylaws should be carefully reviewed to determine the specific maintenance responsibilities of the condominium association and the co-owners.

Site Condominium Projects

Site condominium projects are composed of single-family homes, and each unit is typically composed of land as opposed to airspace. The physical appearance of a site condominium is often no different from a traditional subdivision composed of single-family homes; however, as discussed below, site condominiums and traditional subdivisions are governed by different legal frameworks. While the term "site condominium" does not exist in the Michigan Condominium Act, Michigan courts have recognized that site condominiums may be created under the Act and have defined them as follows:

> The "condominium unit" of a site condominium is typically the home itself and is defined as the "portion of the condominium project designed and intended for separate ownership and use." MCL 559.104(3). The "general common elements" are usually the private roads used by the owners to gain access to the public roads, and the term is defined as "the common elements other than the limited common elements." MCL 559.106(5) .... Most site condominium developments have exactly the same wide-ranging ramifications as traditionally platted subdivisions.

Stanley Bldg Co v St Clair Shores, unpublished per curiam opinion of the Court of Appeals, issued July 27, 2004 (Docket No. 245168), p 2.

Business Condominium Projects

Business condominium projects are created primarily for commercial use and often contain professional office space, industrial complexes, or retail stores. In Michigan, a business condominium unit has a specific definition. MCL 559.103(5) defines a "business condominium unit" as a unit within a condominium project with a sales price of more than $250,000 and is offered, used, or intended to be used for purposes other than residential or recreational purposes. Developers that sell business condominium units are exempt from various requirements under the Michigan Condominium Act that apply to the sale of other types of condominiums. Specifically, when a developer sells a new business condominium unit, they are not required to use the same purchase agreement as a new residential condominium unit, they are not required to provide the same disclosure documents, and the requirements that apply to successor developers also differ.

Accordingly, while the condominium bylaws ultimately determine what condominium units, if any, may be used for commercial use, it is important to note that a condominium unit that is used for a commercial use is not always a "business condominium unit" under the Michigan Condominium Act because the terms "commercial use" and "business condominium unit" are not interchangeable.

Mixed-Use Condominium Projects

Mixed-use condominium projects include a mix of residential and commercial condominium units in a single condominium project. Mixed-use condominiums often have unique governing documents to address the differing interests of the residential and commercial co-owners.

Other Types of Condominium Projects

Other types of condominium projects include the following:

- Airplane hangar condominium projects, in which airplanes are stored and share a common element runway.

- Campsite condominium projects, in which the units are composed of individual campsites.

- Car storage condominium projects, in which cars can be stored and, in some instances, raced around a general common element track.

- Condominium hotels, in which the co-owners typically have the option to stay in their unit for a period of time and rent out the unit on their own or as part of a <u>rental pool</u> for a period of time.

- Dockominiums or marina condominium projects, in which individual boat slips are the units.

- Leasehold condominium projects, in which the co-owners do not own all portions of the condominium but instead lease certain portions of the condominium.

- Mobile home condominium projects, although most mobile home parks are not condominiums.

- RV condominium projects, in which the units often are composed of pads where RVs park and, in some instances, small outbuildings for use by the co-owner in addition to the RV.

Mandatory and Voluntary Homeowners Associations

Michigan does not have a "homeowners association act" to govern the formation of a homeowners association. Instead, subdivisions are established under the <u>Michigan Land Division Act</u>, and a developer (also called a declarant) records a declaration, deed restrictions, or other form of restrictive covenants that attaches to all lots in the subdivision.

Unlike a condominium association, where membership is mandatory, membership in a homeowners association is mandatory only if it is required by the restrictive covenants. Accordingly, membership in some homeowners associations is optional. Most homeowners associations that govern subdivisions are set up as nonprofit corporations and are subject to the <u>Michigan Nonprofit Corporation Act</u>.

Accordingly, almost all homeowners associations must comply with the laws that govern nonprofit corporations; however, it is important to note that even a <u>voluntary or unincorporated homeowners association</u> still has the authority to enforce restrictive covenants.

Differences Between a Site Condominium and Homeowners Associations in Platted Subdivisions

The vast majority of new single-family home developments in Michigan are site condominiums. At first glance, a site condominium project looks a lot like a traditional subdivision; however, there are several key <u>differences between a site condominium and a traditional subdivision</u> because traditional homeowners associations are **not** governed by the Michigan Condominium Act. The key differences include, but are not limited to, the following:

- **Amending Governing Documents**. MCL 559.190 and MCL 559.190a set forth the voting procedures for amending the master deed and condominium bylaws for a Michigan condominium association. Amendments that materially amend the master deed and condominium bylaws require at least 2/3 co-owner approval, and in some instances, 2/3 mortgagee approval. The Michigan Condominium Act does not allow modification of the approval requirements for amending the governing documents.

  In contrast, the declaration of a homeowners association only may be amended as a matter of contract based upon the amendment requirements in the original declaration. Many homeowners association documents set certain time periods during which the governing documents can be amended. If there is no amendment provision in a declaration, then unanimous consent of all lots is required to amend the governing documents.

- **Audits/Reviews**. MCL 559.157 requires a condominium association with annual revenues in excess of $20,000.00 to have its financial statements independently audited or reviewed by a certified public accountant on an annual basis. A condominium association may opt out of having a CPA perform an audit or review of the books, records, and financial statements if a majority of the co-owners approve opting out. While the Michigan Nonprofit Corporation Act requires that condominium and homeowners associations prepare certain financial information each year, there is no statutory requirement that a homeowners association perform an audit or review. Accordingly, homeowners associations are only required to perform an audit or review if required to do so by the governing documents.

- **Common Elements vs. Common Areas**. In a site condominium, the common areas are known as common elements and typically are jointly owned in common by all the co-owners in the condominium. MCL 559.137 states that co-owners have an undivided interest in the common elements based upon the percentage of value assigned to the unit that is identified in the master deed. In a traditional subdivision, the subdivision plat may confer rights on the owners to use certain common areas; however, the common areas in many homeowners associations are owned by the association, not the owners.

- **Developer Turnover**. In a site condominium, MCL 559.152 requires a developer to turn over control of the association's board of directors based on the number of units sold. The Michigan Condominium Act contains a formula that governs how directors are elected to the board of directors during

- A method for equitably allocating expenses between the sub-associations or the owners. By way of example, will expenses be split based on the total number of units in a project, the total number of completed units, equally between the sub-associations, or by another formula?

- Does the master association have to prepare an annual budget and collect assessments?

- How and when will expenses be billed by the master association to the sub-association or the owners? When will those bills be due?

- What penalties exist if a sub-association or owner fails to pay the master association in a timely manner?

Unfortunately, if the governing documents are unclear or the community associations cannot agree on a cost-sharing agreement, the community associations may be forced to pursue litigation to have a court determine their respective responsibilities. In some situations, this may just be a matter of requesting a court to interpret the language of the governing documents. In other situations, the governing documents may simply provide an easement for use, such as for ingress and egress of over roads, but are silent as to how costs are to be allocated. In addressing this type of situation, the Michigan Court of Appeals has held as follows:

> It is the owner of an easement, rather than the owner of the servient estate, who has the duty to maintain the easement in a safe condition so as to prevent injuries to third parties. However, the maintenance costs of an easement used jointly by both the dominant and servient owners are to be paid in proportion to each party's use.

Bayberry Group, Inc v Crystal Beach Condo Ass'n, 334 Mich App 385, 402; 964 NW2d 846 (2020). Accordingly, in the absence of a specific agreement, Michigan courts will conduct a fact-specific inquiry to determine the use by the parties to allocate costs under an easement.

Summer Resort Associations

In addition to traditional homeowners associations, Michigan also recognizes a unique type of homeowners association called a "Summer Resort Association." These are established under one of the following five statutes:

- Act 230 of 1897, Summer Resort and Park Associations, MCL 455.1, et seq.

- Act 39 of 1889, Summer Resort and Assembly Associations, MCL 455.51, et seq.

- Act 69 of 1887, Suburban Homestead, Villa Park, and Summer Resort Associations, MCL 455.101, et seq.

- Act 137 of 1929, Incorporation of Summer Resort Owners, MCL 455.201, et seq.

- Act 161 of 1911, Parks, Playgrounds, Drives, and Boulevards, MCL 455.301, et seq.

Summer Resort Associations are governed by their respective Summer Resort Act and the Michigan Business Corporation Act, MCL 450.1101, et seq. Summer Resort Associations were first created over 100 years ago and are governed by a set of complicated, unique, and archaic rules. By way of example, MCL 445.60 of the

Summer Resort and Assembly Associations Act and <u>MCL 455.214</u> of the Incorporation of Summer Resort Owners Act both state that any person who violates the bylaws "shall be deemed guilty of a misdemeanor, and upon conviction thereof shall be punished by a fine not exceeding 25 dollars or imprisonment in the county jail not to exceed 30 days, or by both such fine and imprisonment in the discretion of the court...." While a criminal penalty for violating restrictive covenants would certainly eliminate many bylaw violation issues, I am not aware of any Michigan court that has jailed anyone for a bylaw violation this century; however, the Michigan legislature made significant updates to the Summer Resort and Park Associations Act in 2022. The major updates to this Act are as follows:

- **MCL 455.3**. The limit on personal property that can be held by a Summer Resort Association was increased from $200,000 to $6,000,000, and this amount will be adjusted for inflation using the Consumer Price Index in the future.

- **MCL 455.9**. The requirement that only stockholders can serve as directors was eliminated. Stockholders can now nominate an immediate family member to serve in their place.

- **MCL 445.10**. The limit on annual expenditures of a Summer Resort Association without stockholder approval was increased from $1,000 to $30,000, and this amount will be adjusted for inflation using the Consumer Price Index in the future.

- **MCL 455.23**. The limit on an increase in special dues without stockholder approval was increased from $25 to $750 in any one year, and this amount will be adjusted for inflation using the Consumer Price Index in the future.

Chapter 2

---✦---

Community Association Operations

There are several items every board will need to address on a regular basis to ensure that the community is run smoothly from year to year. Specifically, association operations can typically be divided into three categories: (1) financial operations, (2) governance, and (3) general operations.

Financial Operations

- Create a budget and levy annual assessments

- Levy additional assessments or special assessments when appropriate

- Implement the association's collection policy

- Conduct regular reserve studies for long-term financial planning

- Obtain a community association loan, if necessary, to fund necessary repairs

- Review or audit financial statements regularly

- File annual tax returns

Governance

- File annual reports

- Hold association and board meetings

- Follow proper procedures to legally act outside of a meeting

- Keep meeting minutes and maintain books and records

Operations

- Obtain advice from professionals to provide additional liability protection

- Enter into contracts with vendors

- Perform necessary maintenance and repairs under the governing documents

- Create written, revocable architectural approvals and modification requests

- Ensure that the association and co-owners have proper insurance

In this chapter, we will break down each of these items and provide brief information on how to manage each of the responsibilities, along with links to more in-depth resources to further help you succeed. A checklist for basic operations that a community association should perform is contained in **Appendix A**.

Financial

Budgeting Different Types of Assessments

One of the most important jobs of a board is to create a budget and levy annual assessments to pay for operations, maintenance, and repairs. Accordingly, while many boards are tempted to keep the assessments low, assessments must be adequate for the board to properly operate the association, provide necessary services, and maintain buildings or common elements in a safe condition.

When creating a budget, Michigan condominium associations are required to set aside money for the creation of a reserve fund. MCL 559.205 and Mich. Admin. Rule 559.511(1) require a condominium association to maintain a reserve fund that is at least 10% of the association's current annual budget on a noncumulative basis. When determining the amount to be earmarked for the reserve fund, associations should be aware that most need to set aside much more than the minimum requirement in order to avoid large additional or special assessments that the co-owners may not be able to afford in the future. As will be discussed below, it is recommended that most condominium associations, particularly ones with attached condominium units, obtain a reserve study on a regular basis to ensure that assessments are sufficient to create an adequate reserve fund and maintain the availability of mortgage financing for potential purchasers. In contrast, a homeowners association is not required to maintain a reserve fund unless required to do so by its governing documents.

All community associations, though, should keep in mind that a budget is just an estimate of anticipated expenses for the year. Accordingly, if unexpected expenses arise, most governing documents permit associations to levy an additional assessment for operating expenses without a vote of the owners. Association boards should not confuse an additional assessment with a special assessment. The differences between additional and special assessments are as follows:

- **Additional assessments**. An additional assessment is authorized by the association's governing documents and allows the association to collect revenue to meet shortfalls in general operating expenses, often to repair or replace existing common elements. Additional assessments can typically be levied by the board without a vote of the owners.

- **Special assessments**. A special assessment is like an additional assessment but differs in several aspects. Most community association bylaws allow for special assessments for additions to common elements over a certain dollar amount, collection of assessments to purchase a unit after foreclosure, or for other purposes not allowed under the additional assessment provisions of the governing documents. Special assessments typically require approval by the co-owners and cannot be levied by the board without a vote of the owners.

Reserve Studies and Reserve Funding

A reserve study is a valuable tool for community associations to utilize in preparing annual budgets and a long-range plan to ensure that the association has adequate funding to maintain the common elements well into the future. An initial reserve study involves an on-site inspection and analysis of the existing reserve fund to prioritize maintenance and repairs over a future time period, often 30 years. The reserve study will then forecast the useful life of the common elements and the estimated cost to repair or replace the common elements in the future. As will be discussed below, a reserve study should be updated periodically to account for any changes in the conditions of the common elements, materials cost increases, or labor cost increases in order to ensure that future association expenses are forecasted as accurately as possible. Conducting regular reserve studies can help you maximize the value of your physical and financial assets and will also let you know if your reserve is underfunded, which will help you adjust your association's long-term financial plans.

Many boards fall into the trap of simply budgeting from year to year and not developing a multi-year plan. While the exact cause of the Surfside condominium collapse in Florida has not yet been determined, there has been a renewed focus across the country on ensuring that community associations do not kick the proverbial can down the road and that a sufficient reserve fund is created for major repairs and replacements. By way of example, the new Freddie Mac Lending Guidelines that were enacted in February 2022, which apply to condominiums with five or more attached units, states as follows with respect to the requirements of reserve studies that they will accept for the purposes of mortgage lending:

1. The reserve study generally must include an inventory of major components of the project, an evaluation of current reserve fund adequacy, and a proposed annual reserve funding plan.

2. A reserve study's financial analysis must validate that the project has appropriately allocated the recommended reserve funds to provide the condominium project with sufficient financial protection comparable to Freddie Mac's standard budget requirements for replacement reserves.

3. The reserve study's annual reserve funding plan, which details total costs identified for replacement components, must meet or exceed the study's recommendation and conclusion.

4. The most current reserve study (or update) must be dated within 36 months of the mortgage lender's determination that a condominium project is eligible.

5. The reserve study must be prepared by an independent expert skilled in performing such studies (such as a reserve

study professional, a construction engineer, a certified public accountant who specializes in reserve studies, or any professional with demonstrated experience and knowledge in completing reserve studies).

6. The reserve study must meet or exceed requirements set forth in any applicable state statutes.

7. The reserve study must comment favorably on the project's age, estimated remaining life, structural integrity, and replacement of major components.

   If the mortgage lender relies on a reserve study that meets the requirements of this section, the project's budget must contain appropriate allocations to support the costs identified in the study.

   The mortgage lender must obtain and retain in the mortgage file a copy of the reserve study. The mortgage lender must also perform an analysis of the study and retain this analysis in the mortgage file.

We recommend that a condominium association with five or more attached units obtain a reserve study and have it updated at least every three years. While there is presently no legal requirement in Michigan that a condominium association obtain a reserve study, it is a best practice to do so in order to prepare an appropriate budget, educate the co-owners on why assessment increases are necessary, maintain the common elements in a safe condition, and maintain property values by making sure that mortgage financing is available to prospective purchasers. Accordingly, condominium associations should consider amending their condominium documents to include requirements that the board of directors obtain, or update, a reserve study at least every three years to ensure that this best practice is followed. While this may result in added expense to the budget, the Surfside condominium collapse demonstrates that this will be money well spent.

Finally, it is important to note that prior to the Surfside condominium collapse, many reserve studies did not include recommendations related to structure of the building. As a result of Surfside, many reserve studies will now include a general structural inspection and, if structural issues are spotted, a referral will be made to a structural engineer to provide recommendations to the condominium association. Accordingly, when hiring a company to perform a reserve study, it is important to understand the scope of the inspection, particularly with respect to inspections and recommendations related to structural items. It is also important to check credentials, as the Community Associations Institute provides <u>credentialling</u> for reserve study specialists.

Community Association Loans

If a community association has never had a reserve study and the reserve fund does not contain sufficient funds to cover expenses of necessary maintenance and repairs, a community association loan may be an option. There are a variety of banks that specialize in community association lending across the country, and this may be an option to fund repairs and maintenance in situations where co-owners may not be able to afford a large additional assessment but would be able to afford incremental assessment increases over time so the association can repay the loan. Unlike a traditional mortgage, community association loans are typically not secured by real estate because the common elements or common areas usually cannot be mortgaged. Similarly, community association loans do not require a lien or mortgage to be placed on individual condominium units or homes. In most cases, community association loans are only secured by future assessment payments.

Generally speaking, Michigan nonprofit corporations have the ability to secure a loan unless doing so is prohibited by the governing documents. The Michigan Nonprofit Corporation Act, specifically MCL 450.2261(1)(i), states as follows:

> A corporation, subject to any limitation provided in this act, in any other statute of this state, or in its articles of incorporation, has the power in furtherance of its corporate purposes to do any of the following:
> …
> Make contracts, give guarantees, and incur liabilities, borrow money at rates of interest as the corporation may determine, issue its notes, bonds, and other obligations, and secure any of its obligations by mortgage or pledge of any of its property or an interest in the property, wherever situated. …

If your community association is looking into obtaining a loan, the board of directors should review the governing documents to determine if the board has the authority to obtain a loan or if a vote of the owners is required. Some governing documents permit the board of directors to obtain a loan without a vote of the owners while others require varying levels of approval, generally somewhere between 51%-75% owner approval.

Community association loans are appealing to banks because they have a low default rate; however, banks do not provide community association loans unless specific underwriting requirements are met. While underwriting requirements may be slightly different depending on the bank, common requirements that must be met to secure a community association loan are as follows:

- **Delinquency Rate**. Most banks will require that less than 7-10% of all units in the project be behind on their assessment payments and not be more than 60 days past due.

- **Litigation.** Most banks will not provide loans to associations that are involved in significant litigation that has unknown potential liability. Some banks will provide loans to associations in litigation that is largely over equitable relief and when there is not a significant financial risk to the community association.

- **Increase in Assessments**. In most cases, community associations will need to agree to increase assessments and maintain assessments at a certain level in order to pay back the loan over time.

- **Owner Occupancy**. Many banks would like at least 80% of the units in the condominium to be owner-occupied. Generally speaking, if a condominium is less than 60% owner-occupied, the bank may not approve a loan because the risk of defaulting increases if units are heavily-owned by investors.

In order to verify the above requirements will be satisfied, along with any other requirements of the bank, it is a good idea to gather the information in our lending checklist contained in **Appendix B** to prepare for the lending process.

Review and Audits of Financial Statements

MCL 559.157 requires a Michigan condominium association with an annual revenue in excess of $20,000 to have its financial statements independently audited or reviewed by a certified public accountant on an annual basis; however, a condominium association may vote to opt out of having a CPA perform an audit or review of the association's financials if a majority of the co-owners approve opting out.

A homeowners association does not have to perform an audit or review unless it is required to do so in its governing documents; however, a homeowners association that is a Michigan nonprofit corporation is required to prepare financial statements and provide the most recent financial statement to a homeowner upon request, similar to a condominium association.

Tax Returns

Although most community associations are nonprofit corporations, they are required to file tax returns every year. Generally speaking, a community association has three different filing options: (1) Federal Form 1120-H, (2) Federal Form 1120, or (3) Federal Form 990.

In most cases, a community association utilizes the 1120-H form. This is a simple, single-page form that is designed for associations that derive their income from assessments, which is classified as exempt income. To qualify for Federal Form 1120-H, at least 60% of the association's income must qualify as exempt. Even though filing community association tax returns is relatively simple, we still recommend that a community association hire a CPA to prepare and file the tax return in order to ensure it is properly done, even if the association does not owe any taxes.

Governance

Annual Reports

At least once each year, associations that are organized as corporations must file an annual report with Michigan's Department of Licensing and Regulatory Affairs ("LARA") to maintain their corporate status. Pursuant to MCL 450.2911, nonprofit corporations are required to file annual reports with LARA by October 1st of every year. The annual report notifies the public that the corporation continues to exist and of the names of the current directors and officers, as well as the identity of the current resident agent who accepts service on behalf of the corporation.

If a corporation fails to file an annual report for a period of two years from the date that an annual report was due to be filed, it may be <u>automatically dissolved</u> by LARA; however, MCL 450.2925(1) permits a corporation to renew its corporate status by filing annual reports for the last five years, or any lesser number of years that the reports were not filed, along with paying the annual fees and a $5.00 penalty for each annual report. Once the annual reports are filed, MCL 450.2925(2) states that the rights of the corporation are the same as if the dissolution had not taken place and all contracts entered into and acquired during that time period are valid and enforceable.

Association Meetings

Association meetings cover a wide range of topics and issues. As you conduct these meetings, you will need to understand and follow these guidelines:

- **Meeting Notice**. Pursuant to MCL 450.2404, each member is entitled to receive notice of an association meeting no less than 10 days but not more than 60 days before the meeting. The notice must be in writing and may only be delivered electronically if the member has consented to receiving electronic notice. We generally recommend that an association create a standard template that each co-owner can complete to document that they consent to receiving electronic notice so owners can obtain information faster and the association can reduce its postage costs.

- **Quorum**. To transact association business, the association must meet <u>quorum</u> requirements. This entails holding an annual association meeting, typically in the spring or fall, with significant attendance by members in order to elect directors, distribute financial statements, and provide all appropriate updates.

- **Voting**. Generally speaking, members in a community association are entitled to vote at an association meeting. The eligibility to vote is determined based on the record date. Pursuant to MCL 450.2412, if the bylaws do not identify a record date, the board may set a record date that is not less than 10 days and not more than 60 days before the meeting. If the board does not set a record date, the record date is the close of business on the day next preceding the day that notice of the meeting is given. Governing documents also commonly disqualify a member from voting if they are delinquent in paying their assessments.

  Similarly, it is important to review the condominium documents to determine if votes are cast in number, percentage of value, or both. In Michigan, every condominium unit must be assigned a <u>percentage of value</u>. In addition to determining the undivided ownership interest of a co-owner in the common elements, the percentage of value is sometimes used to determine the voting power or assessment obligations of a co-owner. Accordingly, if a vote is required to be passed by a majority of co-owners in number and in value, it is important to ensure that votes are properly tabulated because it is possible that a vote could pass in number but not in value.

- **DVRs and Proxies**. To help meet quorum requirements or to further their own agendas (or both), prior to an annual or special meeting, you will often see board candidates or other members soliciting the right to vote on behalf of other members. If a member cannot attend a meeting, they may want to allow someone else to temporarily vote as their proxy; however, it is important to understand the difference between a

DVR and proxy. Unlike a proxy, a DVR, or designated voting representative, is the person who permanently receives all notices and votes on behalf of the unit. Accordingly, members that unknowingly complete a DVR, as opposed to a proxy, may unwittingly give away important rights, such as receiving notices from the association or voting rights. Ensure that your members are informed of this difference so that they can make an informed decision regarding who can vote in their stead in the event they cannot attend one or more meetings.

- **Electing Officers and Directors**. In most community associations, the same individuals serve as officers and directors, but these are two different roles and it is important that associations understand the difference between them. With a few exceptions, the directors of the association are elected by the members at an annual meeting of the association. Generally, the association is controlled by its board of directors and a majority vote of the board of directors is necessary for the association to act. On the other hand, officers, such as the president, vice president, secretary, and treasurer, are appointed by the board of directors. The authority of officers is limited to the specific powers delegated to the officers by the bylaws or by the board of directors. The bylaws set the requirements to serve as an officer or director. Generally, directors must be members of the association, but many bylaws permit non-members to serve as officers of an association.

- **Differences Between Board Decisions and Member Decisions**. Another common issue that community associations encounter is whether certain decisions are made by the board of directors or a vote of the members. While the governing documents for each community association are different, in most associations, there are very few decisions that are made by the owners at a meeting. In many community association documents, members may elect directors, remove directors, vote to amend the governing documents, or vote to impose a special assessment (not to be confused with the additional or annual assessment that usually does not require a member vote); however, the board of directors makes almost all other decisions in a community association.

- **Parliamentary Procedure**. Robert's Rules of Order, or some other form of parliamentary procedure, should be used for maintaining uniformity and order at all association and board meetings. This is a set of rules for conduct at meetings that gives everyone a chance to be heard without confusion. In some cases, the governing documents may contain a specific order of business; however, if they do not, then we recommend that you consult with a community association attorney to help you prepare a meeting agenda and learn the basics of parliamentary procedure. While it is good form to follow Robert's Rules of Order, minor deviations from parliamentary procedure are unlikely to invalidate otherwise valid actions taken at a meeting.

Aside from these details, your board, officers, and members should all be aware that if quorum requirements are not met for an election, then the current directors can carry over their positions until an election is held.

While annual meetings traditionally are conducted with all participants physically present, in most cases Michigan law allows members to participate in meetings through electronic means. The Michigan Nonprofit Corporation Act, specifically MCL 450.2405(1), provides, in pertinent part, "unless otherwise restricted by the articles of incorporation or bylaws, a shareholder, member, or proxy holder may participate in a meeting of shareholders or members by a conference telephone or other means of remote communication that permits all persons that participate in the meeting to communicate with all other participants."

Therefore, a member not physically present at an association meeting may participate by means of remote communication and still be considered present. Thus, this person may vote if all the following conditions are met:

- The corporation implements reasonable measures to verify that each person considered present and permitted to vote at the meeting by means of remote communication is a member or proxy holder.

- The corporation implements reasonable measures to provide each member or proxy holder a reasonable opportunity to participate in the meeting and to vote on matters submitted to the members, including an opportunity to read or hear the proceedings of the meeting substantially concurrently with the proceedings.

- If any member or proxy holder votes or takes other action at the meeting by means of remote communication, a record of the vote or other action must be maintained by the corporation.

Board Meetings

The first step in holding a board meeting is to provide proper notice to the board members under the bylaws. <u>Board meetings may be limited in terms of attendance to only board members,</u> who are the only ones entitled to receive a notice regarding board meetings. While association meetings require the participation of members, board meetings do not. <u>Michigan's Open Meetings Act</u> and <u>Freedom of Information Act</u> do not apply to association board meetings because a community association is not a "public body." Thus, board meetings are not required to be open to all members unless this requirement is contained in the bylaws; however, many boards exercise their discretion to have certain portions of board meetings open to the membership to obtain feedback from the members.

Taking Action Outside of a Meeting

In many cases, the governing documents permit a community association to vote outside of a meeting, which is often known as an "action without meeting." The Michigan Nonprofit Corporation Act, specifically MCL 450.2408, permits an action without meeting provided the following requirements are satisfied:

- The articles of incorporation or bylaws permit a vote by ballot outside of a meeting.

- The ballot provided to the members sets forth the proposed action, provides an opportunity for each member to vote for or against each action, and the ballot specifies a time to return the ballot that is not less than 20 days or more than 90 days after the date on which corporation provides the ballot to the members.

Accordingly, it is common for community associations to vote on matters outside of a meeting, especially in situations such as during the COVID-19 pandemic. Finally, some associations may choose to hold voting at a specified polling place, which could include online voting options. To do this, though, your articles of incorporation or bylaws need to permit voting at a polling place.

Meeting Minutes

The Michigan Nonprofit Corporation Act, specifically MCL 450.2485, states that "[a] corporation shall keep books and records of account and minutes of the proceedings of its shareholders or members, board, and executive committee, if any." Accordingly, all community associations that are nonprofit corporations are required to keep meeting minutes. Generally speaking, the meeting minutes should contain the following items, unless different items are required by the bylaws:

- Identify the type of meeting being held, such as an association meeting or board meeting.

- Identify the legal name of the community association.

- Identify the date, time, and location of the meeting.

- Identify the presiding officer that called the meeting to order.

- Perform a roll call and identify the board members in attendance, if it is a board meeting, and any other persons present.

- Document that quorum was established at both association and board meetings.

- Document any reports that were given and who provided the report; however, keep in mind that these are minutes, not hours, so keep the description brief.

- Document the vote to approve the prior meeting minutes because minutes are only in draft form until approved.

- Document any votes that took place at the meeting under new business.

- Document any votes that took place at the meeting under old business.

- Identify the time that the meeting was adjourned.

The meeting minutes need not record every conversation that happened at the meeting. Rather, the meeting minutes should reflect any votes that took place at the meeting and a record of who voted for or against any matter that was voted on. Associations must keep these records in written form or in a form that can be reasonably converted to written form (e.g., in a digital format that can be printed).

Books and Records

In addition to keeping meeting minutes, the Michigan Nonprofit Corporation Act requires associations to maintain a balance sheet, statement of income for the fiscal year, and a membership list. Similarly, the administrative rules of the Michigan Condominium Act require a condominium association to keep a book of mortgagees. While this is not an exhaustive list of records a community association should keep, an association should be aware of the minimum statutory requirements for record keeping.

If a member entitled to inspect your records requests them, a nonprofit corporation must convert the records to written form and provide them to the person or make them available for inspection, depending on the types of records being requested. Pursuant to MCL 450.2487, a nonprofit corporation must mail a member, if requested in writing, a "balance sheet as of the end of the preceding fiscal year; its statement of income for that fiscal year; and, if prepared by the corporation, its statement of source and application of funds for that fiscal year."

A member must also articulate a proper purpose for inspecting all other books and records and there are certain exemptions to record inspections. Nevertheless, if a board does receive a proper request that complies with all the statutory requirements, then MCL 450.2487 requires the association to permit an inspection within five business days, although the inspection itself does not necessarily have to occur within this timeframe. MCL 450.2487 defines a proper purpose as a "purpose that is reasonably related to a person's interest as a shareholder or member." Even if the condominium bylaws do not contain a "proper purpose" requirement to inspect association records (because none is required under the Michigan Condominium Act), the Michigan Court of Appeals has recognized that a proper purpose is still necessary if the community association is a nonprofit corporation:

> ...MCL 450.2487(2) and (3) explicitly condition a right to examine records on having a "proper purpose" for so doing. The Condominium bylaws and MCL 559.157(1) do not, but because legally vindicating a frivolous or vexatious request would at least theoretically be impossible, we think that a "proper purpose" is nevertheless an implicit condition of making any such request to examine records. Additionally, "our courts have recognized a stockholder's common-law right to inspect corporate records for a proper purpose," noting that a proper purpose might include "raising doubts whether corporate affairs had been properly conducted by the directors or management" but would not include "requests to satisfy idle curiosity or aid a blackmailer" or "mere *speculation* of mismanagement." *North Oakland Co Bd of Realtors v Realcomp, Inc*, 226 Mich App 54, 58–59; 572 NW2d 240 (1997). At its heart, the development of legal rights such as this one has always been for the purpose of providing people with tools to maintain order and decorum, not to provide people with swords with which to create chaos and harm.

Vidolich v Saline Northview Condo Ass'n, unpublished per curiam opinion of the Court of Appeals, issued Dec 5, 2017 (Docket No. 334579), p 7.

Given that a court can potentially award attorney's fees and costs if an owner prevails in a lawsuit if a community association wrongfully denies an inspection, it is important to consult with a community association attorney to evaluate inspection requests. This is especially true if a community association plans to deny a request to inspect records.

Director Duties

A director or officer of a condominium association owes a fiduciary duty to act in the best interest of the association. Michigan courts have defined a fiduciary duty as follows:

> .... a fiduciary duty generally requires one to "act for someone else's benefit, while subordinating one's personal interests to that of the other person" (internal citation, quotation marks, and emphasis omitted). In addition, a fiduciary owes its principal a duty of good faith, loyalty, and avoidance of self-dealing.

Baughman v W Golf & Country Club, Inc, unpublished per curiam opinion of the Court of Appeals, issued June 9, 2009 (Docket No. 279425), p 1.

The Michigan Nonprofit Corporation Act, specifically MCL 450.2541, provides the standard of care for a director or officer of a nonprofit corporation and provides, in pertinent part:

> A director or officer shall discharge his or her duties as a director or officer including his or her duties as a member of a committee in the following manner: (a) In good faith (b) With the care an ordinarily prudent person in a like position would exercise under similar circumstances (c) In a manner he or she reasonably believes is in the best interests of the corporation.

Pursuant to the <u>business judgment rule and MCL 450.2541</u>, directors and officers can rely on information, opinions, reports, or statements from experts. This may include financial statements and data prepared or presented by the following:

- Another director, officer, or employee of the association whom the director or officer reasonably believes to be reliable and competent in advising on the subject matter.

- Other experts, including legal counsel, engineers, or public accountants.

However, if the director or officer has knowledge on the matter in question that makes reliance on an opinion or report unwarranted, then the director or officer is **not** entitled to rely on that information.

Conflicts of Interest

Community association boards frequently encounter awkward situations in which a fellow board member has a potential conflict of interest, such as hiring a company a board member owns or works for, approving an architectural request of a board member, or pursuing a bylaw violation against a board member. If managed properly, potential conflicts of interest can be easily navigated. While it is easiest if an interested board member recuses themself from any transaction, this is not always legally required. The Michigan Nonprofit Corporation Act, specifically MCL 450.2545a, states that interested director provisions will be set aside, or not give rise to damages, if at least one of the following circumstances exists:

- The transaction was fair to the corporation at the time it was entered into.

- The material facts of the transaction and the director's or officer's interest were disclosed or known to the board or an executive committee of the board, and the board or executive committee authorized, approved, or ratified the transaction by an affirmative vote of the majority of the directors or executive committee that did not have an interest in the transaction.

- The material facts of the transaction and the director's or officer's interest were disclosed or known to the shareholders or members who are entitled to vote, and they authorized, approved, or ratified the transaction by an affirmative vote of the majority of the members that did not have an interest in the transaction.

Finally, to avoid and resolve conflicts of interest, many community association boards will include specific provisions relating to these issues in their bylaws or adopt a code of conduct as part of their rules and regulations. Examples of common topics that are addressed include:

- Creating procedures for recusing interested directors and officers from transactions in which they may have an interest.

- Prohibiting directors, officers, or volunteers from receiving goods, services, or items of value from community association vendors, other than small or nominal gifts.

- Disclosing or prohibiting transactions in which a director, officer, volunteer, or any of their family members would receive a direct or indirect financial benefit if the community association hired a certain vendor.

- Preventing individual directors, officers, or volunteers from directing the work of a contractor for their own personal benefit without approval from the board of directors.

Operations

Architectural Approvals and Modification Requests

Owners often want to make modifications and improvements to their individual units or to common elements of the condominium. In most cases, the governing documents will require approval from a community association's board of directors for these modifications. It is important that the bylaws clearly spell out what types of <u>modifications</u> require association approval and if approval is required from the board of directors or an architectural control committee.

If association approval is required for a modification, it is important that written modification agreements are executed that specifically delineate the terms of approval. Common issues that are addressed in a modification agreement are as follows:

- Seeking approval of specific designs or plans to confirm that the modification will not significantly alter the aesthetics of the community.

- Requiring the co-owner to obtain building permits and comply with any other municipal ordinances or state laws.

- Identifying the party responsible for the cost of installation, maintenance, and repair of the modification.

- Requiring the owner to indemnify the association for any damage to person or property caused by the modification.

- Identifying whether the approval is permanent or revokable and whether a subsequent purchaser will be entitled to rely on the modification approval.

Accordingly, a written modification agreement protects the owners against a new board that might try to pursue action against them for violating the bylaws, perhaps years later. Further, this practice helps a community association avoid unnecessary additional responsibility or risk resulting from modifications.

Contracts

Failing to properly perform due diligence prior to hiring contractors and failing to thoroughly review your community association's contracts may lead to significant legal issues. All contracts should be in writing and contain the following important provisions:

- The parties to the contract

- Scope of goods or services provided

- Time for performance

- Length of the contract and how it can be renewed

- Compensation

- Insurance requirements

- Indemnification and hold harmless provisions in favor of the association

- Termination provisions

- Whether the contracts can be assigned or transferred

- Whether the contract can be cancelled due to force majeure, an act of God, or other unforeseen events such as the coronavirus pandemic

- An integration clause indicating that the written agreement is the entire agreement

- A process for amending the contract in writing

It is not necessary for legal counsel to review every single contract for a community association; however, many community associations have counsel draft a form contract that can be used with multiple vendors. It is advisable, though, for an attorney to review major contracts and long-term contracts that could have a major impact on a community association's operations or expose it to significant liability if the contract is breached.

Maintenance and Repair

As a result of the Surfside condominium collapse, there has been an increased focus on maintenance in community associations, particularly in attached condominiums. Generally speaking, most governing documents will require that a community association maintain the common elements or common elements of a building in order to protect the safety of the co-owners and maintain property values. Some governing documents contain specific maintenance standards, and the board of directors should maintain the community association according to any standards set forth in the governing documents and ensure that sufficient assessments are collected to do so.

In addition to complying with the governing documents, it is important that the association performs regular maintenance on the common elements in order to maintain eligibility for mortgage financing. In 2022, both Fannie Mae and Freddie Mac issued new lending guidelines indicating that they would stop providing mortgages to purchasers of condominium units in certain communities if certain maintenance standards were not met. Unfortunately, Fannie Mae and Freddie Mac have also indicated that lenders may impose additional underwriting requirements that relate to maintenance. Generally speaking, community associations will be asked to complete a questionnaire related to the condition of the condominium, among other things, if a purchaser of a condominium unit is obtaining a mortgage. Based on the current lending guidelines, condominiums with five or more units that have significant maintenance issues, which are more fully identified in **Appendix C**, will be ineligible for most traditional mortgage financing. In order to demonstrate that a condominium is being properly maintained, lenders will generally request copies of meeting minutes, reserve studies, or engineering reports.

Professional Property Management

Operating a community association can be a time-consuming task and, in some cases, can easily end up being a full-time job. As with learning anything new, it will typically take more time for somebody who is not experienced in operating a community association. Generally speaking, a professional property management company will assist the board of directors in handling the following types of tasks:

Administrative Management

- Investigating violations of the governing documents and sending an initial warning letter requesting corrective actions

- Maintaining the association's books and records

- Responding to requests from owners

- Preparing mailings and notifications to owners

- Preparing proposed agendas for annual and board meetings

- Recommending the association to obtain legal advice on important decisions

- Attending association and board meetings

Financial Management

- Collecting assessments, depositing funds into the association's bank account, and maintaining owner ledgers

- Assessing late fees and sending initial delinquency notices prior to turning over an account to the association's attorney

- Paying bills from the association's bank account

- Preparing financial reports and coordinating with the association's accountant to prepare audits, reviews, and tax returns

- Recommending an annual budget for the board of directors to approve

- Obtaining quotes for association contracts, such as contractors, professional services, and insurance

- Providing payoffs to title companies when units are transferred

- Processing insurance claims

Physical Management

- Inspecting the common elements and common areas for necessary maintenance and repairs

- Recommending maintenance and repairs to the board of directors

- Maintaining the common elements and common areas pursuant to any standards in the governing documents and directions of the board of directors

- Keeping maintenance and repairs records

- Receiving and responding to owner requests for maintenance, including emergency repairs

- Ensuring that basic utilities are provided to the building

Some community associations opt to be self-managed. While self-management may save money, it typically creates more work for the volunteer board members as evidenced by the lengthy list of tasks outlined above. Similarly, the savings that result from not having to pay a management fee may be offset if the directors do not have the knowledge, time, or skill set to appropriately handle owner complaints or bid out contracts for vendors. A management company can also be useful in maintaining historical knowledge and records if the board members frequently change. Other associations will opt for a hybrid form of self-management and professional management, where a management company is hired to perform certain tasks. In a hybrid management situation, a management company will often perform only financial services and the board of directors will perform the administrative and physical services. Many associations, though, will opt for full-service professional property management. While full-service property management will add additional costs to the annual budget, the value provided over self-management often outweighs the cost savings because many board members do not have the time or experience to perform full self-management. Accordingly, every board needs to decide whether professional management best suits the needs of their community with the understanding that the needs of the community may change over time.

Finally, if a community association opts out of self-management, it is recommended that the association's attorney review the management contract because it will be one of the most important contracts that the association will enter into and it is often a multi-year contract. Accordingly, it is important that the scope of the contract be appropriately outlined, to identify whether the obligations within the contract can be assigned to another management company without the consent of the association, and to ensure the appropriate insurance provisions are included, along with outlining termination procedures that are fair to both sides if the relationship does not work out over the long-term.

Insurance

Duties of the Insurance Carrier

Every insurance contract imposes two separate duties on an insurance carrier, the duty to defend and the duty to indemnify. The duty to defend requires an insurance carrier to pay for an attorney to defend a claim that may potentially be covered under the insurance policy. The Michigan Court of Appeals has explained the duty to defend as follows:

The duty of the insurer to defend the insured depends upon the allegations in the complaint of the third party in his or her action against the insured. This duty is not limited to meritorious suits and may even extend to actions which are groundless, false, or fraudulent, so long as the allegations against the insured *even arguably* come within the policy coverage. An insurer has a duty to defend, despite theories of liability asserted against any insured which are not covered under the policy, if there are any theories of recovery that fall within the policy. The duty to defend cannot be limited by the precise language of the pleadings. The insurer has the duty to look behind the third party's allegations to analyze whether coverage is possible. In a case of doubt as to whether or not the complaint against the insured alleges a liability of the insurer under the policy, the doubt must be resolved in the insured's favor.

Citizens Ins Co v Secura Ins, 279 Mich App 69, 74–75; 755 NW2d 563 (2008).

Accordingly, the duty to defend is extremely broad and, if a claim, or any part of a claim, could potentially be covered under an insurance policy, the insurance company must provide a defense; however, if the claim clearly falls within an exception under an insurance policy, the insurance company is not required to provide a defense and it may deny the claim.

The duty to indemnify requires an insurance carrier to pay a loss under an insurance policy, such as a judgment, so long as the loss is covered by the insurance policy and within policy limits. Similarly, if there is no lawsuit pending, the duty to indemnify is only triggered if there is a covered loss under an insurance policy. Accordingly, unlike the duty to defend, in order for the duty to indemnify to be triggered, the claim must be covered by the insurance policy, as opposed to *arguably* be covered by the insurance policy. As such, the duty to indemnify is narrower than the duty to defend.

Insurance Requirements for Condominium Associations

A condominium association is required to have general liability insurance to cover damage to person or property. MCL 559.156 of the Michigan Condominium Act also states, in pertinent part, that a condominium association's bylaws may contain provisions "for insuring the co-owners against risk affecting the condominium project, with prejudice to the right of each co-owner to insure his condominium unit or condominium units on his own account and for his own benefit." Mich. Admin. Rule 559.508 addresses a condominium association's requirement to carry insurance and states as follows:

> The bylaws shall provide that the association of co-owners shall carry insurance for fire and extended coverage, vandalism and malicious mischief, and, if applicable, liability and workers' disability compensation, pertinent to the ownership, use, and maintenance of the premises and that all premiums for insurance carried by the association shall be an expense of administration. The association may carry other insurance coverage, including cross-coverage for damages done by 1 co-owner to another.

The insurance requirements for a condominium project are largely dictated by the master deed and condominium bylaws. In addition to the mandatory property insurance coverage, most condominium documents will also require one or more of the following types of insurance coverage:

- General Liability Insurance

- Property Insurance

- Directors and Officers Insurance

- Crime & Fidelity Insurance

- Cyber Insurance

- Worker's Compensation Insurance

- Homeowners Insurance (maintained by individual owners)

Depending on the type of condominium project being insured and the language of the condominium documents, the association and co-owners will have different insurance requirements, both in terms of policy limits and coverage.

Insurance Requirements for Homeowners Associations

In the context of homeowners associations, there are no laws that require a homeowners association to carry insurance because Michigan does not have a statute governing homeowners associations. Accordingly, the insurance requirements, if any, in a homeowners association are dictated by the governing documents. Generally speaking, homeowners associations will have similar types of insurance as outlined above; however, homeowners associations that are composed of single-family homes, as opposed to attached units, will typically have less insurance responsibilities under the governing documents because there are typically fewer common areas to insure.

General Liability Insurance

All community associations should have a general liability insurance policy, which is commonly known as a commercial general liability or CGL insurance policy. A CGL insurance policy will typically cover claims for negligence related to bodily injury (such as a slip and fall), property damage, and other types of personal injury claims (such as libel, slander, or advertising injury). The board of directors should review the governing documents to determine if there is a minimum coverage amount and consult with their insurance agent to determine an appropriate amount of coverage. Also, it is recommended that community associations ensure that they have an "occurrence"-based insurance policy as opposed to a "claims made"-insurance policy. An "occurrence"-based policy provides coverage for claims that occurred during the policy period, even if the claim is not filed during the policy period. In contrast, under a "claims made"-policy, the insurance company only has to provide coverage if the occurrence happened during the policy period **and** the claim was submitted during the policy period.

Property Insurance

Property insurance provides coverage for common elements and common areas against physical loss or damage from fire, storms, natural disasters, and other occurrences. By way of example, if a fire burned down a portion of a condominium, the property insurance policy would provide coverage to rebuild the structure and any other common elements of the condominium. In some cases, a community association is required to provide insurance coverage for the individual units as well, but in most modern community association documents, the individual owners will be required to obtain their own insurance, as discussed further below.

A community association board should consult with their insurance agent to determine an appropriate amount of coverage. As a general rule of thumb, it is important that a property insurance policy cover the actual replacement cost of all buildings. Moreover, in evaluating property insurance policies, community associations should be aware that there are typically three levels of coverage that are available that will vary in costs:

- **"All In" Insurance Coverage**. "All In" coverage is the broadest form of coverage. "All In" property insurance will cover common elements and fixtures within a unit, such as appliances, cabinets, floor coverings, and wall coverings, which are not personal property. "All In" insurance covers upgrades made to a condominium unit as well. If the condominium association documents also require a unit owner to obtain insurance for their individual unit, it will typically create a situation where there is overlapping coverage with an "All In" insurance coverage policy. Accordingly, it is important that the condominium bylaws have a clause that identifies whether the community association or individual owner's insurance policy will provide primary coverage.

- **"Single Entity" or "Walls In" Insurance Coverage**. Many community associations will have a "Single Entity" or "Walls In" insurance policy, which is similar to an "All In" insurance policy, except that it does not provide coverage for upgrades that were made to a condominium unit.

- **"Bare Walls" Insurance Coverage**. A "Bare Walls" insurance policy offers the least amount of insurance coverage from a community association perspective because it only covers the drywall itself and provides no insurance coverage for the interior of a unit. If there is a flood or fire, a "Bare Walls" insurance policy does not pay for fixtures within a unit, such as appliances, cabinets, floor coverings, and wall coverings, or any upgrades to a unit. Rather, these items would be covered under the unit owner's HO-6 insurance policy.

If the governing documents require a specific type of coverage, a community association should obtain the type of property insurance coverage required by the governing documents. If the governing documents do not require a specific type of property coverage, a community association board should consult with their attorney and insurance agent to determine the best type of coverage for their particular circumstances.

Finally, while various endorsements exist that can be added to most community association property insurance policies, three of the most important that board members should discuss with their insurance agents, which may also impact whether Fannie Mae and Freddie Mac will provide loans within a particular community association, are as follows:

- **Boiler and Machinery / Equipment Endorsement**. A boiler and machinery or equipment endorsement covers a loss from mechanical or electrical systems within a building. Generally speaking, this type of endorsement will cover boilers, water heaters, solar heaters, pressure pipes, elevators, and generators from losses, other than normal wear and tear. Fannie Mae and Freddie Mac typically require this endorsement for lending purposes if there is central heating ventilation and cooling system in a building.

- **Building and Ordinance Endorsement**. A building and ordinance violation endorsement is important because it will provide coverage to rebuild an entire building, if required by municipal ordinance, even if all of the building was not damaged. By way of example, if a building had a fire and 75% of the building was destroyed but the remaining 25% of the units were not damaged, the municipal ordinance may require the entire building to be demolished. A building and ordinance endorsement would provide coverage to demolish and rebuild 100% of the building to comply with the municipal ordinance, even though 25% of the units were not damaged. Similarly, this endorsement would cover upgrades required by ordinance, such as a fire suppression system. Finally, a building and ordinance endorsement is also important because both <u>Fannie Mae</u> and <u>Freddie Mac</u> require that that certain types of condominium associations have this endorsement in order to lend in the community.

- **Inflation Guard Endorsement**. An inflation guard endorsement provides that the amount of insurance will automatically increase by a certain percentage each year or that an increase will occur based on an index. If the prices of materials increase significantly, an inflation guard endorsement will ensure that there is sufficient coverage to rebuild a building. In cases where the property insurance is required to cover 100% of the full replacement cost, an inflation guard endorsement may not be necessary.

Directors and Officers Insurance

Every community association should maintain a directors and officers insurance policy, often referred to as D&O insurance. While D&O insurance, like any insurance, does not cover all potential lawsuits, it does provide a defense and indemnity for many claims against a community association, directors, officers, committee members, employees, volunteers, and property managers. Accordingly, it is unwise to serve on a community association board without confirming whether a D&O insurance policy exists and without reviewing the D&O policy to determine what types of claims are covered. Generally speaking, a D&O insurance policy will cover claims related to decisions or "wrongful acts" made by directors, offers, committee members, employees, volunteers, or property managers. Examples of common types of claims that are covered under a D&O insurance policy include:

- Adoption of rules

- Architectural control decisions

- Assessment decisions

- Breach of fiduciary duty

- Defamation

- Election disputes

- Failing to enforce bylaws

Similar to property insurance, though, there are typically two different types of D&O policies which offer different levels of coverage. Generally speaking, what is known as a "package policy," which is combination of different types of insurance packaged together and sold at a lower price, will cover the above items; however, the following types of claims may be excluded under a "package policy" but may be covered under a standalone D&O insurance policy, which is not packaged with other types of community association insurance:

- Claims for non-monetary damages (i.e., injunctive and declaratory relief)

- Claims for failing to purchase appropriate insurance

- Defense costs for breach of contract claims

- Discrimination / fair housing claims

- Employment practices claims

- Insured versus insured claims (i.e., one board member suing another board member)

Generally speaking, a standalone D&O insurance policy will provide broader coverage than a "package policy." Accordingly, it is important to consult with the association's attorney and insurance agent to determine which type of insurance policy is best for a particular community.

Crime and Fidelity Insurance

Crime and fidelity insurance protects a community association from certain types of criminal acts. Examples of claims that may be covered under a crime and fidelity insurance policy are:

- Employee dishonesty, such as theft by board members, officers, committee members, employees, volunteers, bookkeepers, or property managers that have access to association funds

- Forgery

- Theft of personal property

- Counterfeiting

- Wire fraud

By way of example, if a board member made unauthorized cash withdrawals and embezzled funds from the community association, a crime insurance policy would reimburse the community association for its loss and the insurance company would be responsible for attempting to recoup any missing funds from the board member. If a community association does not have crime insurance and cannot recover stolen funds, it may lead to large additional assessments against the members and interfere with general association operations.

Crime insurance is not always included in a community association's master insurance policy. Accordingly, board members should consult with their insurance agent to determine if they are adequately covered. In some cases, the governing documents will require a fidelity bond as opposed to crime insurance; however, coverage under a fidelity bond is typically much narrower than under a crime insurance policy because it typically only covers specific directors, officers, or a property management company.

In addition to protecting a community association's assets, it is also important to know that <u>Fannie Mae</u> and <u>Freddie Mac</u> require certain types of condominium associations to carry crime insurance to meet mortgage underwriting requirements. While there are several exceptions, generally speaking, if an association has more than $5,000 in funds and more than 20 units, it will need to have crime and fidelity insurance to meet mortgage underwriting guidelines. As a general rule, the crime and fidelity policy must provide coverage for dishonest or fraudulent acts for anyone that is responsible for handling association funds, including the property manager. The lending guidelines also indicate that a property manager should be covered by their own crime and fidelity insurance. Fannie Mae and Freddie Mac also require crime and fidelity insurance coverage that insures the maximum funds that are in the control of the association or property management company at any one time. If certain financial controls are in place, then the crime and fidelity coverage may be reduced to a minimum sum of three months of assessments on all units in the project; however, even with financial controls in place, it is prudent to obtain crime insurance that would cover a complete loss of the association's funds.

Cyber Insurance

Unfortunately, crime and fidelity insurance policies do not always cover all types of crime or only provide a limited amount of coverage. Given that cybercrime is on the rise, a community association may also need a standalone cyber insurance policy to adequately protect itself from cybercrimes. This is especially true because volunteers typically run community associations and can be viewed as easy targets for cyber criminals. Examples of cybercrime that may be covered under a cyber insurance policy include:

- Data breaches if a board member, officer, volunteer, or property manager loses a computer or cell phone or personal information is accidentally leaked to the public

- Computer hacking, when third-parties hack into data kept by an association, such as bank account or credit card information

- Cyber extortion, when data is stolen and kept for a ransom after inadvertently clicking on a link in a phishing email

- Identify theft

- Social engineering, i.e., creating a fake email pretending to be a board member and authorizing the distribution of funds

While cyber insurance is relatively new and coverage will vary from policy to policy, items that can be covered under a cyber insurance policy include:

- Legal and forensic services to determine if a data breach occurred

- Expenses to notify community association members impacted by a cybercrime

- Expenses related to restoring data or a network

- Regulatory defense costs and fines for violations of privacy regulations

- Crisis management and public relations expenses

- Damages related to an interruption of association operations or to restore association funds lost as a result of a cybercrime

- Cyber extortion reimbursement

- Judgments from third parties that have suffered a loss after a data breach

Accordingly, community associations that are responsible for protecting data for association members, accept electronic payments, or allow board members or property managers to keep sensitive date online or on their electronic devices should consider purchasing a standalone cyber insurance policy.

Workers' Compensation Insurance

Workers' compensation insurance provides coverage for an employee if they are hurt or injured in work-related accidents. In

Michigan, an employer is required to carry workers' compensation insurance if it regularly employed one or more employees for at least 35 hours a week for at least 13 weeks during the last year or an employer has more than three employees at any time. In other cases, a community association's governing documents require it to carry workers' compensation insurance. Generally speaking, a worker's compensation insurance policy will cover the following types of work-related injuries:

- Replacement wages

- Medical expenses

- Death benefits

Even if an association is not required to carry workers' compensation insurance because it has no employees, many community associations will still carry a workers' compensation policy for additional liability protection. First, certain types of workers' compensation insurance policies will provide coverage to directors, officers, or volunteers. Accordingly, if your association has volunteers that help with landscaping or perform any type of maintenance and they are injured while engaged in these activities, a workers' compensation policy may provide coverage. Second, an association may hire an uninsured co-owner to provide maintenance, fail to check the insurance of a contractor, or be unaware that a contractor has failed to pay their workers' compensation insurance or let a policy lapse. If the association had some degree of control over the activity that caused an injury, the injured party may attempt to argue that the association was an employer and entitled to worker's compensation benefits.

Finally, in addition to liability issues, there are significant penalties in Michigan if an employer fails to carry workers' compensation insurance. Specifically, an employer may be subject to a fine of $1000 or imprisonment for no less than 30 days or more than six months, or both, if a court determines that an employer failed to carry workers' compensation insurance and was legally required to do so. Each day that an employer fails to carry workers' compensation insurance is a separate offense. Accordingly, if an association does not have workers' compensation insurance and forgets to obtain a policy after hiring its first employee, or it is later determined that the association was in fact an employer, even if it did not believe it had entered into an employment relationship with a particular individual, the association and directors could be subject to significant penalties. Given that workers' compensation insurance is relatively inexpensive, it is a best practice for community associations to carry a workers' compensation policy, even if they are not legally required to do so.

Homeowners Insurance

Michigan does not require homeowners to carry insurance, but most mortgage lenders do. Similarly, many governing documents require owners to carry insurance on their unit. The insurance policy obtained by a co-owner that occupies a unit in a condominium is often referred to as an HO-6 policy. An HO-6 policy covers items such as personal property and other obligations that the co-owner is responsible for under the governing documents; however, it is important to note that most insurance companies will not issue an HO-6 policy to a co-owner that does not occupy the unit. Rather, if the co-owner rents the unit, an insurance company will issue a DP-3 insurance policy, which offers less coverage than an HO-6 policy.

Chapter 3

--- ✦ ---

Transitioning the Association from Developer Control to Owner Control

Every condominium association in Michigan goes through a transition phase, also known as a "turnover." During this phase, the control of the condominium association shifts from the developer to the co-owners. The process of this transition in condominium associations is governed by the Michigan Condominium Act.

Because the Michigan Condominium Act does not govern homeowners associations, during the transition period, homeowners associations are governed solely by the governing documents. While homeowners association board members may gain some insights from this chapter on procedures that are likely included in their governing documents, we will focus specifically on condominium associations.

At times, the transition process may seem complicated, but a successful turnover is crucial to the future success of your condominium association. In this chapter, we will provide information and resources to guide you through a successful turnover.

Hold a Transitional Control Meeting to Elect Co-Owner Directors

Transitioning control from the developer over to the co-owners starts with holding an annual meeting to elect co-owner directors. MCL 559.152 provides the following requirements for electing co-owner directors to the association's board of directors:

- Not later than 120 days after conveyance of legal or equitable title to non-developer co-owners of 25% of the units that may be created, at least 1 director and not less than 25% of the board of directors of the association of co-owners shall be elected by non-developer co-owners. Not later than 120 days after conveyance of legal or equitable title to non-developer co-owners of 50% of the units that may be created, not less than 33-1/3% of the board of directors shall be elected by non-developer co-owners. Not later than 120 days after conveyance of legal or equitable title to non-developer co-owners of 75% of the units that may be created, and before conveyance of 90% of such units, the non-developer co-owners shall elect all the directors on the board, except that the developer shall have the right to designate at least 1 director as long as the developer owns and offers for sale at least 10% of the units in the project or as long as 10% of the units remain that may be created.

- Notwithstanding the formula provided in subsection (2), 54 months after the first conveyance of legal or equitable title to a non-developer co-owner of a unit in the project, if title to not less than 75% of the units that may be created has not been conveyed, the non-developer co-owners have the right to elect, as provided in the condominium documents, a number of members of the board of directors of the association of co-owners equal to the percentage of units they hold and the developer has the right to elect, as provided in the condominium documents, a number of members of the board equal to the percentage of units which are owned by the developer and for which all assessments are payable by the developer.

Pursuant to MCL 559.110(7), the official transitional control date is the date on which a board of directors is elected in which the votes cast by the co-owners unaffiliated with the developer exceed the votes which may be cast by the developer. It is not uncommon for developer-controlled condominium associations to fail to elect directors in compliance with the Michigan Condominium Act. This can cause significant issues down the line and can impact the operation of the condominium association. Therefore, your first order of business in the turnover process is to hold the developer accountable for calling a meeting in a timely manner and electing a co-owner-controlled board of directors.

Developer Turnover Checklist

After the transitional control date, when a majority of the board is composed of co-owners, the association will want to ensure that the rest of the transition process proceeds smoothly. Here is a turnover checklist that outlines best practices that should take place after the transitional control date:

1. **Perform an initial audit of the documents provided by the developer**. A condominium association board should have all association books and records, including, but not limited to, the following:

   • The master deed, condominium bylaws, and all recorded amendments

   • The developer's disclosure statement, which is typically part of a purchaser information booklet

- The articles of incorporation, including any amendments

- A complete set of association and board meeting minutes

- All rules and regulations

All accounting information, including all financial statements, audits, and reviews

- All records related to escrow funds for "must be built" improvements and any performance bonds

- The current operating budget and all prior operating budgets

- All bank accounts, including the reserve funds, and banking records

- All reserve studies that have been performed

- All state and federal tax returns

- All insurance policies

- All contracts entered into by the association

- A complete list of all current co-owners with addresses and any other contact information

- All co-owner files, including ledgers related to assessment payments for each co-owner, approvals related to construction, and modification approvals

- All site plans, including any as-built drawings

- A list of all contractors, manufacturers, subcontractors, and suppliers involved with the project, as well as any warranty information

- All documents related to any past or pending claims

- The association's tax identification number

2. **Retain a certified public accountant**. A qualified CPA should be enlisted to perform an audit or review of the association's financials. It is not uncommon for a developer to comingle funds with the development prior to the transitional control date. Accordingly, a CPA can review an association's finances to ensure that the developer has made appropriate financial contributions to the association as required by the governing documents and to ensure that the developer has not used the association's funds to subsidize its operations.

3. **Hire a property management company**. It is common for the developer-controlled board of a condominium association to hire a third-party professional management company; however, in some cases, the developer or its affiliates function as the management company. The Michigan Condominium Act, specifically MCL 559.155, permits the board to void a management contract with the developer or affiliates of the developer within 90 days of the transitional control date or with 30 days' notice any time thereafter for cause. If the contract extends beyond one year, the board may shorten the contract by providing appropriate notice as well. Often, if the management company is a third-party company, it remains so even after the transition because the company has institutional knowledge of the association's operations; however, the co-owner-controlled board will need to evaluate whether to self-manage the condominium association, continue on with

the existing management company, or hire a new management company.

4. **Hire a reserve study professional**. Unfortunately, many developers do not have a reserve study completed prior to the transitional control date. Accordingly, for many condominium associations, the first time that a reserve study takes place is after the transitional control date. A reserve study is essential to accurately setting assessments. Prior to the developer transitional control date, many developers simply set assessments to fund bare minimum association operations, but a reserve study will help the board set an appropriate budget and prepare a long-range plan. In some cases, the same company may be able to perform a reserve study and an inspection to search for construction defects, as discussed further below; however, not all reserve study specialists are willing or able to serve as experts in construction defect litigation. Similarly, not all construction defect experts are qualified to prepare reserve studies. Accordingly, the board should make sure that it clearly defines the scope of work and ensures that it has an appropriately-qualified professional perform a reserve study.

5. **Hire a civil engineer**. An association should have a licensed civil engineer inspect all the common elements of the condominium project to look for readily-apparent and hidden construction defects. Examples of common construction defects in new construction condominiums include:

- Collapsing retaining walls resulting from improper installation

- Cracking in the foundation or drywall caused by concealed foundation issues

- Improperly-installed electrical wiring within common element walls

- Flooding or drainage issues caused by improper installation of underground storm water drainage systems

- Heaving or cracking of concrete porches, driveways, or sidewalks due to poor drainage

- Leaks, mold, and other water-related issues caused by improperly-installed roofing, siding, flashing, or windows

- Noise related to insufficient insulation and poor sound protection

- Burst pipes resulting from a failure to insulate common element pipes

- Premature road failure resulting from failure to test or account for soil conditions, improper use of base course materials, or drainage issues

- Missing or improperly-installed trusses, which compromise the structural integrity of the roofing or building

The engineer should prepare a report outlining any construction defect, the cause of the defect, a proposed fix, whether any of the problems are covered by warranty, and the estimated cost to fix the problems. This report will assist the board and the condominium association's attorney in evaluating the scope of the problems and determining the best course of action.

6. **Hire a community association attorney**. Once the transitional control date is reached, the board should hire an attorney on behalf of the association. MCL 559.276 provides a condominium association with three years from the transitional control date or two years from the date that a claim accrues to pursue a construction defect claim arising out of

the development or construction of a condominium project. In cases of fraudulent concealment (that is, when the developer appointees on the board hide construction defects), a court may extend the statute of limitations.

A claim for breach of contract against a contractor for a defect that arises from the repair or replacement of a construction defect that is not related to the initial development of the condominium typically has a six-year statute of limitations. Accordingly, given the shorter statute of limitations that applies to claims that arise out of the development of a new condominium, an association should act quickly to improve its odds of success in pursuing a developer. Similarly, many developers often attempt to get new co-owner boards to sign releases for simply fulfilling their statutory obligations. Accordingly, legal counsel should be retained if the association is presented with such an agreement to ensure that the association's interests are protected.

Do You Have Any Construction Defects?

If a civil engineer finds construction defects in the condominium, the engineering report should identify all the defects in the project and include proposed fixes and cost estimates.

In Michigan, the responsibility for construction defects in a new condominium project is most often attributable to the developer. While there are various theories of liability that can be used to pursue a developer, the most common theory is based on the implied warranty of habitability. Under the implied warranty of habitability, a developer warrants that the common elements were properly constructed and turned over to the co-owners in good working order. The Michigan Court of Appeals has described the implied warranty of habitability in a condominium as follows:

There were two types of transfers of property that occurred in relation to the development. The first type of transfer was the transfer of the individual units. Many such transfers occurred and each transfer was completed pursuant to the purchase agreement. Consequently, each of those transfers is subject to the terms of the purchase agreements....

The second apparent type of transfer that occurred in relation to the development was the transfer of the control and possession of the common areas from the developer to the Association. This transfer was not completed pursuant to the purchase agreement. We conclude that implied warranties are created when a developer-vendor transfers common areas to an Association. In *Smith v Foerster-Bolser Construction, Inc*, 269 Mich App 424, 431; 711 NW2d 421 (2006), this Court held that an implied warranty of habitability is created when a developer-vendor transfers a new home to a purchaser. In *Plymouth Pointe Condominium Ass'n v Delcor Homes-Plymouth Pointe, Ltd*, unpublished opinion of the Court of Appeals, issued October 28, 2003 (Docket No 233847), this Court noted that other jurisdictions have held that the same warranty of habitability also applies to the development and purchase of new condominiums *and the accompanying common areas* (see *Berish v Bornstein*, 437 Mass 252; 770 NE2d 961 (Mass, 2002). Such a rule is logical and necessary. If this Court were to accept defendants' logic, developers could routinely avoid liability for defective common areas by inserting disclaimers into the purchase agreements of the individual homeowners. Associations would be left without a remedy, despite the fact that they were not parties to the purchase agreements.

Heritage in the Hills Homeowners Ass'n v Heritage of Auburn Hills, LLC, unpublished per curiam opinion of the Court of Appeals, issued Feb 2, 2010 (Docket No. 286074), pp 9–10.

Before holding a developer responsible for construction defects, a condominium association must identify the identity of the "developer," which may prove to be difficult in certain cases. The Michigan Condominium Act, specifically MCL 559.106(2), defines a developer of a condominium as "a person engaged in the business of developing a condominium as provided in this act."

While real estate brokers and residential builders are, in certain circumstances, excluded from the definition of a "developer" under the Michigan Condominium Act, the definition of a developer is extremely broad and often may encompass more than one person or corporate entity. In many cases, you will need to enlist the help of your community association attorney to ensure that you identify the correct entities that are liable for the cost of <u>resolving condominium project defects</u> because developers often advertise under a trade name, use one entity as a land-holding company, and then use another entity or other contractors to perform construction. Similarly, in failed condominium projects, successor developers may have liability for taking over a condominium project because MCL 559.235 requires a successor developer to comply with the Michigan Condominium Act in the same manner as the original developer and to fulfill express written warranties of the original developer.

In some cases, the former developer appointees who served on the association's board of directors will also have personal liability if they breached their fiduciary duties to the association by making decisions for the association that benefited the developer's interest at the expense of the association; however, the fact that a developer appointee is engaged in self-dealing, in and of itself, is not sufficient to establish a claim of breach of fiduciary duty. Liability is only triggered when the transaction involving self-dealing was also unfair to the corporation.

Has the Developer Completed All "Must Be Built" Items?

MCL 559.203b(3) states that a developer is required to maintain an escrow fund in connection with the purchase of each unit until all the following occurs:

- Issuance of a certificate of occupancy for the unit, if required by local ordinance.

- Conveyance of legal or equitable title of the unit to the purchaser.

- Receipt by the escrow agent of a certificate signed by a licensed professional engineer or architect either confirming that those portions of the phase of the project in which the condominium unit is located and which are labeled "must be built" are substantially complete or determining the amount necessary for substantial completion thereof.

- Receipt by the escrow agent of a certificate signed by a licensed professional engineer or architect either confirming that recreational or other facilities which are labeled "must be built," whether located within or outside of the phase of the project in which the condominium unit is located and those which are intended for common use, are substantially complete or determining the amount necessary for substantial completion thereof.

Whether due to ignorance, the tedious and expensive nature of fulfilling the above requirements, or some combination of both, many developers do not comply with MCL 559.203b. This is something to watch out for in the turnover process because a vast majority of disclosure statements indicate that funds are held in escrow, even when they may not be.

Alternatively, MCL 559.203b(5) allows for a developer to opt out of maintaining an escrow fund, which would need to be properly disclosed in the disclosure statement and escrow agreement, if they provide the escrow agent with "evidence of adequate security, including, without limitation, an irrevocable letter of credit, lending commitment, indemnification agreement, or other resource having a value, in the judgment of the escrow agent, of not less than the amount retained pursuant to subsection (3)."

Many developers do not provide a letter of credit or lending commitment because this exposes them to additional liability if the "must be built" structures and common elements are not completed. Additionally, if a developer goes out of business and fails to complete the project, then an indemnification agreement does little to ensure that the condominium project is completed. Thus, it is important to ensure that all "must be built" common elements and units have been completed so the association is not left with a partially-completed project.

Is the Condominium Properly Configured? Have Any "Need Not Be Built"

The Michigan Court of Appeals has provided much-needed guidance in addressing issues related to incomplete "need not be built" units that determine the configuration of the condominium. MCL 559.167 originally was enacted to provide an end date for the development of condominium projects. MCL 559.167(3) initially required a developer and its successors or assigns to either complete any units identified as "need not be built" on the condominium subdivision plan within 10 years of the date of commencement of construction of the project or within six years of exercising a right of conversion, expansion, or contraction of the project.

If the developer and its successors or assigns failed to complete the "need not be built" units or withdraw them from the project within the statutory time periods, then the right to construct the units was automatically terminated and the undeveloped land remained as common elements owned by all the co-owners.

In 2016, though, amendments to MCL 559.167 created a new "reversion" process to eliminate "need not be built" units after the expiration of the six or 10-year statutory time periods. Newly-created MCL 559.167(4) requires 2/3 of the co-owners who are in good standing to vote to approve a "reversion" of "need not be built" units to common elements by adopting a declaration that will be recorded in the register of deeds after the expiration of the statutory time periods.

If 2/3 co-owner approval is obtained, then the condominium association must send the declaration to the developer or successor developer at its last known address. The developer or successor developer may withdraw the land on which the units were to be located or amend the master deed to make the units "must be built" within a 60-day period.

If the developer or successor developer fails to withdraw the land or amend the master deed within 60 days, then the condominium association may record the declaration, which becomes effective upon recording, and the developer or successor developer loses the right to construct those "need not be built" units.

In _Cove Creek Condo Ass'n v Vistal Land & Home Dev, LLC,_ 330 Mich App 679, 685; 950 NW2d 502 (2019), the Michigan Court of Appeals issued a published opinion establishing binding legal precedent and clear guidance on the interpretation and application of MCL 559.167. In _Cove Creek, supra,_ the Court of Appeals decided the following important issues:

- MCL 559.167, as amended in 2016, cannot be used to retroactively re-create "need not be built" condominium units that ceased to exist by operation of law prior to September 21, 2016, when MCL 559.167 was last amended.

- MCL 559.167, as amended in 2002 and as it existed prior to September 21, 2016, was constitutional, and the loss of a developer's or successor developer's right to construct units due to the passage of time did not violate the due process or takings clauses of the Michigan or United States Constitutions.

Given that the *Cove Creek* decision is binding precedent, attorneys, co-owners, condominium associations, developers, successor developers, and title companies should be aware of the following in the turnover process:

- MCL 559.167, as amended in 2002, applies to **all** condominium projects that existed at the time the statute was enacted, not just condominium projects that were created on or after the effective date of 2002 PA 283.

- "Need not be built" condominium units are automatically eliminated by operation of law under MCL 559.167, as amended by 2002 PA 283, and a replat or recording of any additional documents is not necessary.

- The co-owners acquire vested rights in the common elements under MCL 559.167, as amended by 2002 PA 283, which cannot be eliminated by 2016 PA 233.

- The co-owner voting "reversion" process and the additional 60-day time period for a developer to withdraw "need not be built" units that was created in 2016 only applies to condominium projects in which the six or 10-year statutory periods did not expire by September 21, 2016 or to condominium projects created after September 21, 2016.

Did the Developer Properly Set Up Recreational Facilities?

Recreational facilities in condominium projects – such as barbeques, basketball courts, boat slips, clubhouses, gyms, parks, picnic areas, pools, private lakes, saunas, spas, or tennis courts – often are some of the amenities most attractive to potential buyers. Many recreational facilities are common elements located within a condominium project and may only be used by the co-owners. In these situations, the recreational facilities are controlled solely by the condominium association's board and the maintenance, repair, and upkeep of the recreational facilities are financed through assessments collected pursuant to MCL 559.169.

Some recreational facilities located in condominium projects, though, may also be used by third parties. It is also common for a developer to build recreational facilities on a property located outside of the condominium project that is used by multiple condominium projects or apartment complexes. Situations involving recreational facilities that are not solely owned and controlled by the co-owners are often more complicated because the interests of the co-owners may differ from the third parties that either own or use these facilities.

Accordingly, the Michigan Condominium Act and accompanying administrative rules have specific requirements that must be satisfied when a condominium association shares its recreational facilities with third parties or when the co-owners utilize recreational facilities that are owned by a third party. MCL 559.234 states that "recreational facilities and other amenities, whether on condominium property or on adjacent property with respect to which the condominium has an obligation of support, shall comply with requirements prescribed by the administrator, to assure equitable treatment of all users." Mich. Admin. Rule 559.111 sets forth the requirements that must be satisfied when third parties utilize recreational facilities owned by the co-owners:

- Disclosure shall be made to all prospective purchasers that the recreational facilities will be shared with a third party.

- The master deed shall define who is entitled to use the recreational facilities.

- The master deed shall set forth the appropriate financial obligations of all the parties involved.

To comply with Mich. Admin. Rule 559.111(a), the disclosure statement for the condominium project must disclose to potential purchasers that the recreational facilities can be used by third parties.

In contrast, Mich. Admin. Rule 559.111 sets forth the following requirements that must be satisfied when the co-owners are obligated to financially support recreational facilities that are owned by third parties:

- Disclosure shall be made to prospective purchasers of their financial obligations and responsibilities as co-owners to support the recreational facilities. Such disclosure shall include information regarding all fees charged and compensation paid.

- The condominium co-owners shall have an equitable vote, as set forth in the disclosure statement, as to the operation and management of the recreational facilities.

- An arbitration clause to settle disputes upon consent of the parties shall be included in the condominium legal documents.

- The necessary easements shall be established.

- The books and records of the recreational facilities shall be kept separate from other operations and shall be made available for inspection by the co-owners.

Accordingly, condominium associations should ensure that the developer or other third parties follow the applicable rules that relate to recreational facilities.

Has the Developer Paid Its Proportionate Share of Expenses or Assessments?

Assessments are determined based on the budget set for the upcoming year. Accordingly, once the overall expenses of the community association are estimated, a budget is created and the amount of the overall expenses contained in the budget is apportioned among the co-owners, either according to percentage of value or any other formula contained in the condominium documents, to determine the assessments that each unit pays.

Many developers, however, pay only a proportionate share of expenses, which is calculated differently from assessments because it is based on actual expenses, as opposed to a budget, and billed to the developer after the expenses are actually incurred. The developer's obligation to pay assessments or a proportionate share of expenses is largely determined by the condominium bylaws, but it is also subject to the requirements contained in MCL 559.169 of the Michigan Condominium Act.

Did the Developer Fund the Reserve at Turnover?

Before concluding the turnover phase, you should ensure that the developer has funded the condominium association's reserve fund. Mich. Admin. Rule 559.511 imposes the following requirements related to reserve funds:

- The bylaws shall provide that the association of co-owners shall maintain a reserve fund for major repairs and replacement of common elements. The association shall maintain a reserve fund that, at a minimum, is equal to 10% of the association's current annual budget on a noncumulative basis.

- The reserve fund required shall only be used for major repairs and replacement of common elements.

- The reserve fund shall be established on the transitional control date. The developer shall be liable for any deficiency in this amount at the transitional control date.

- The following statement shall be contained in the bylaws: "The minimum standard required by this section may prove to be inadequate for a particular project. The association of co-owners should carefully analyze their condominium project to determine if a greater amount should be set aside, or if additional reserve funds should be established for other purposes."

If the developer does not fund the reserve fund adequately, you will need to ensure that the developer is held accountable. Similarly, moving forward, the association will need to impose assessments at a level that will allow an adequate reserve fund to accumulate over time.

Chapter 4

------ ✦ ------

Enforcing the Governing Documents

Every community association has governing documents, which establish the following:

- The contractual relationship between the developer and community association.

- The contractual relationship between each owner and the community association.

- The contractual relationship between each of the owners.

- A corporate governance structure for the community association.

- A mechanism to impose assessments to fund community association operations.

- A set of restrictions on property use that are intended to enhance property values and to protect the health, safety, and welfare of the community.

In the context of a condominium association, the governing documents are typically composed of the master deed, condominium bylaws (which are often referred to as Exhibit A to the master deed), condominium subdivision plan (which is often referred to as Exhibit B to the master deed), articles of incorporation, corporate bylaws (if separate from the condominium bylaws), and any rules and regulations. In the context of a homeowners association, the governing documents typically refer to the recorded declaration or restrictive covenants, articles of incorporation, corporate bylaws, and any rules and regulations. Accordingly, enforcing the governing documents plays a key role in successfully operating a community association. In this chapter, we will outline steps to fairly and consistently enforce the association's governing documents, discuss common violations, and review options for enforcing the governing documents.

The Governing Documents Are Restrictive Covenants That Run with the Land

In *Conlin v Upton*, 313 Mich App 243; 881 NW2d 511 (2015), the Michigan Court of Appeals defined a restrictive covenant as follows:

> A covenant affecting the use of real property runs with the land if, in relevant part, the parties express their intent to bind their successors and assigns. If the covenants are structured to run with the land, a subsequent purchaser will be bound by the covenants if he or she purchases the land with actual or constructive notice of the covenants. A subsequent purchaser is on constructive notice that his or her use of the property will be subject to the covenants when the covenants appear in the purchaser's chain of title.

Accordingly, in condominium projects, the master deed and condominium bylaws constitute restrictive covenants that run with the land. In traditional subdivisions, many associations have a recorded declaration that constitutes a covenant that runs with the land.

What does it mean for a covenant to "run with the land?" It means that an owner is automatically bound by the restrictive covenants that are recorded in the register of deeds, thus providing notice of the covenants to the public, and that they automatically become obligated to comply with the covenants by purchasing and acquiring title to the property. Similarly, it means that a purchaser of real property that is subject to restrictive covenants is responsible for bringing the property into compliance and correcting any violations that the previous owner left.

In Fox Pointe Ass'n v Ryal, unpublished per curiam opinion of the Michigan Court of Appeals, issued July 23, 2019 (Docket No. 344232), the Michigan Court of Appeals addressed the issue of whether a purchaser was responsible for pre-existing violations that were caused by a previous owner. The court held that the purchaser was responsible for the pre-existing violations because the covenants ran with the land and the purchaser inherited the responsibility for correcting any violations caused by the previous owner. Accordingly, associations can hold owners accountable for violating restrictive covenants, even if the violation was created by the prior owner, because the covenants run with the land.

The Governing Documents Must Be Enforced as Written

In Michigan, the master deed and condominium bylaws for a condominium association must be enforced based upon their plain language. In _Tuscany Grove Ass'n v Peraino_, 311 Mich App 389, 393;

875 NW2d 234 (2015), the Michigan Court of Appeals set forth the applicable principles of interpreting restrictive covenants as follows:

> Pursuant to the Condominium Act, the administration of a condominium project is governed by the condominium bylaws. MCL 559.153. Bylaws are attached to the master deed and, along with the other condominium documents, the bylaws dictate the rights and obligations of a co-owner in the condominium. See MCL 559.103(9) and (10); MCL 559.108. Condominium bylaws are interpreted according to the rules governing the interpretation of a contract. Accordingly, this Court begins by examining the language of the bylaws. Words are interpreted according to their plain and ordinary meaning. Further, this Court avoids interpretations that would render any part of the document surplusage or nugatory, and instead this Court gives effect to every word, phrase, and clause. Ultimately, we enforce clear and unambiguous language as written.

In the context of condominiums, the Michigan Condominium Act expressly permits an association or co-owner to bring an action to enforce the plain language of the condominium documents. Specifically, MCL 559.207 provides the following:

> A co-owner may maintain an action against the association of co-owners and its officers and directors to compel these persons to enforce the terms and provisions of the condominium documents. In such a proceeding, the association of co-owners or the co-owner, if successful, shall recover the costs of the proceeding and reasonable attorney fees, as determined by the court, to the extent that the condominium documents expressly so provide. A co-owner may maintain an action against any other co-owner for injunctive relief or for damages or any combination

thereof for noncompliance with the terms and provisions of the condominium documents or this act.

Additionally, MCL 559.215 states, in pertinent part, the following:

> A person or association of co-owners adversely affected
> by a violation of or failure to comply with this act,
> rules promulgated under this act, or any provision of
> an agreement or a master deed may bring an action
> for relief in a court of competent jurisdiction. The
> court may award costs to the prevailing party.

Accordingly, both a condominium association and a co-owner have the ability to enforce the governing documents.

In the context of restrictive covenants for homeowners associations, the Michigan Court of Appeals applied the same principles and reached the same result in _Mazzola v Deeplands Dev Co LLC, unpublished per curiam opinion of the Court of Appeals, issued July 25, 2019 (Docket No. 343878)_. Specifically, the Michigan Court of Appeals held the following:

> …Courts must apply unambiguous restrictive cove-
> nants as written unless the restriction contravenes law
> or public policy,or has been waived by acquiescence
> to prior violations. The general rule with regard to
> interpretation of restrictive covenants is that where
> no ambiguity is present, it is improper to enlarge or
> extend the meaning by judicial interpretation.

Accordingly, it is important that a community association board enforce the documents as written. Often, community association boards fall into the trap of not enforcing the governing documents because of the following reasons: (1) the governing documents were not enforced by the prior board, (2) the current board does not want to spend the money to enforce the governing documents, (3) the board does not want to cause turmoil in the neighborhood, or (4) the board believes that a particular covenant is not fair; however, none of these are legitimate reasons for failing to enforce the covenants as written.

Failing to enforce the governing documents may expose a community association to liability and the directors and officers to claims for breach of fiduciary duty. Thus, if a community association board has an issue with enforcing the plain language of the governing documents, then the best course of action is to amend the governing documents. Similarly, fair and consistent enforcement of the documents will avoid a potential claim by owners of selective enforcement.

As with any general rule, there are certain exceptions to enforcing the plain language of the governing documents. Examples of these exceptions include the following:

- **Fair Housing**. The Federal Fair Housing Act prohibits discrimination based on color, disability, familial status, national origin, race, religion, or sex. Accordingly, if a community association has a restriction that discriminates against a protected class, then it should not be enforced.

- **FCC Rules**. As part of the Telecommunications Act of 1996, the Federal Communications Commission (FCC) adopted the OTARD (Over-the-Air Reception Devices) Rules, which effectively prevent community associations from completely prohibiting owners from installing satellite dishes on areas over which they exercise exclusive control, such as balconies or patios; however, the rule does allow community associations to set certain rules regarding satellite dishes. Accordingly, even if a community association wishes to prohibit satellite dishes, the association should not enforce such a provision to avoid a violation of the OTARD rules.

- **Illegality**. The board is not responsible for enforcing governing documents that were enacted illegally or otherwise violate the law. By way of example, MCL 559.190(2) states the following, in pertinent part:

> Except as provided in this section, the master deed, bylaws, and condominium subdivision plan may be amended, even if the amendment will materially alter or change the rights of the co-owners or mortgagees, with the consent of not less than 2/3 of the votes of the co-owners and mortgagees. A mortgagee shall have 1 vote for each mortgage held. The 2/3 majority required in this section may not be increased by the terms of the condominium documents, and a provision in any condominium documents that requires the consent of a greater proportion of co-owners or mortgagees for the purposes described in this subsection is void and is superseded by this subsection.

> If the condominium bylaws required ¾ of the co-owners' approval for a material amendment, such a provision would be illegal and unenforceable.

- **Equity**. In some very <u>specific cases</u>, the terms of the governing documents are not required to be enforced if certain circumstances can be established, such as waiver. While this is a highly fact-specific inquiry, waiver may apply in the following situations: (1) technical violations and absence of substantial injury, (2) changed conditions, or (3) limitations and laches; however, associations should review their governing documents to determine if they contain an "anti-wavier" clause because Michigan courts have upheld the validity of these provisions and found that waiver had not been established due to a prior failure of an association to enforce the governing documents.

- **Expiration**. In the context of condominiums, the master deed and condominium bylaws generally do not have any type of expiration date and run with the land indefinitely. In the context of declarations for platted subdivisions, there are some restrictions that expire after a set number of years or are required to be renewed after a certain number of years. Similarly, Michigan has a law called the Marketable Record Title Act, MCL 565.01, et seq., which requires certain types of restrictive covenants to be renewed if they do not show up in the chain of title for a particular property in the past 40 years. Prior to 2018, a deed could simply indicate that a property was "subject to all restrictions of record" in order to indicate that a property was bound by the restrictive covenants during the 40-year time period. The Marketable Record Title Act was amended in 2018 and it introduced a requirement that a deed specifically identify any restrictive covenants that bind the property with information sufficient to find the restrictive covenants in the register of deeds. In 2020, the Michigan legislature amended the Marketable Record Title Act to permit property owners, as well as community associations, to record documents in the register of deeds that contain the specific information required by statute to preserve the restrictive covenants until March 29, 2024. In 2022, HB 6730 was enacted by the Michigan Legislature and it amended the Marketable Record Title Act to bar the extinguishment of any "land or resource use restriction." Accordingly, it is important for board members to consult with an attorney about whether action should be taken to preserve the existing restrictive covenants, and whether such action is still necessary after the 2022 amendment to the Marketable Record Title Act.

Generally speaking, all governing documents should be enforced as written and inconsistent enforcement should be avoided whenever possible. If you intend to deviate from enforcing the governing documents as written or if it is questionable as to whether a certain provision is enforceable based on the above exceptions, then the board should consult with a qualified community association attorney to determine the appropriate course of action.

Common Enforcement Problems

While community association restrictions vary from community to community, many associations deal with similar issues. As the Michigan Court of Appeals previously noted in _Cohan v Riverside Park Place Condo Ass'n Inc (After Remand)_, 140 Mich App 564, 569, 570; 365 NW2d 201 (1985):

> Inherent in the condominium concept is the principle that to promote the health, happiness, and peace of mind of the majority of the unit owners since they are living in such close proximity and use facilities in common, each unit owner must give up a certain degree of freedom of choice which he might otherwise enjoy in separate, privately owned property.

The most common bylaw violations that we deal with on a regular basis are identified below, which often arise when co-owners do not understand that they must give up certain freedoms when living in a community association.

Commercial Use Restrictions

Many condominium bylaws and declarations contain a prohibition on the commercial use of a unit or lot. In _Terrien v Zwit_, 467 Mich 56; 648 NW2d 602 (2002), the Michigan Supreme Court defined "commercial use" as follows:

> "Commercial" is commonly defined as "able or likely to yield a profit." _Random House Webster's College_

Dictionary (1991). "Commercial use" is defined in legal parlance as "use in connection with or for furtherance of a profit-making enterprise." Black's Law Dictionary (6th ed). "Commercial activity" is defined in legal parlance as "any type of business or activity which is carried on for a profit." *Id.* "Business" is commonly defined as "a person ... engaged in ... a service." *Random House Webster's College Dictionary* (1991). "Business" is defined in legal parlance as an "activity or enterprise for gain, benefit, advantage or livelihood." Black's Law Dictionary (6th ed).

Thus, a prohibition on commercial use typically is quite broad and includes activities ranging from operating a typical business to using a unit for <u>short-term rentals</u>; however, many documents contain an exception for home-based businesses with no customers. Accordingly, community association boards should carefully review their documents to determine which types of commercial activity, if any, are permitted under the governing documents. It is not uncommon, though, for a community association board to take enforcement action against an owner who attempts to use a condominium unit or lot to operate a business.

Landscaping

Many community associations have landscaping restrictions, including prohibiting an owner from planting trees, flowers, or shrubs or from placing any ornamental materials, including, but not limited to, statuary, bird feeders, exterior lighting, fountains, furniture, implements, rocks or boulders, fencing, or other decorative items without prior board approval. Unfortunately, owners frequently install landscaping without permission, which can drastically alter the aesthetic appearance of the neighborhood over time. Notably, most governing documents contain provisions that require owners to maintain the appearance of their units according to certain minimum standards. Accordingly, it is important for a community association board to enforce these types of violations because they can lower property values in the neighborhood.

Noise, Nuisance, and Illegal Activity

Living in close quarters often creates issues among neighbors. Thus, many governing documents contain a restriction that prohibits any type of illegal activity. By way of example, a restriction on illegal activity can be useful in stopping the short-term rental of a property that is operating in violation of a local municipal ordinance, the violation of a parking ordinance, a home constructed in violation of the building code, or for dealing with somebody smoking marijuana in violation of federal law. Accordingly, the prohibition on illegal activity in community association restrictions is a powerful tool at the board's disposal, especially in situations where an activity may not be expressly prohibited in the governing documents but violates another law.

In addition to prohibiting illegal activity, many governing documents restrict any activity that is unreasonably noisy, a nuisance, dangerous, or unsightly. Accordingly, the board may take enforcement action in situations where an owner hosts loud parties, plays loud music, allows odors to dissipate into other units, or permits smoke to spread to the common areas or other units. While a board can certainly successfully enforce such a provision, the more specific the bylaws are, the better chance the association has of successfully abating a nuisance. By way of example, owners may argue about whether tobacco smoke constitutes a "nuisance," but a community association could certainly amend its governing documents to eliminate smoking and avoid any potential disputes about whether a certain activity constitutes a nuisance.

Parking Issues

The enforcement of parking restrictions is one of the most common problems that community associations are forced to address. Parking spaces often are at a premium in densely packed urban areas, and issues arise when owners fail to park in their designated areas. In contrast, suburban site condominiums with single-family homes often face issues related to parking boats, commercial vehicles, or inoperable vehicles in driveways or on the street. Common parking issues that typically require a board to take enforcement action include the following:

- Owners or their guests parking in prohibited areas.

- Owners parking or storing commercial vehicles, boat trailers, buses, watercraft, boats, motor homes, camping vehicles/trailers, snowmobiles, snowmobile trailers, recreational vehicles, non-motorized vehicles, off-road vehicles, or all-terrain vehicles when they are prohibited by the governing documents.

- Owners who have a greater number of vehicles than permitted by the governing documents.

- Owners who park vehicles on the street or in other areas overnight when they are not permitted to do so.

- Owners who park nonoperational vehicles outside their garage.

In most cases, parking restrictions need to be dealt with through fines, towing, or injunctive relief.

Animal Restrictions

Issues with restrictions regarding animals pose a problem for almost every community association. Common issues involving animals include the following:

- An owner keeping a type of animal that is prohibited by the governing documents.

- An owner having <u>more animals</u> than permitted by the governing documents.

- An owner failing to keep a dog on a leash and the dog bites a child or another owner.

- An owner failing to clean up pet waste.

Accordingly, it is not uncommon for a board to take enforcement action to remove a <u>dangerous animal</u> or ensure that an animal is not causing problems for other owners; however, restrictions on animals must be reasonable and the Michigan Court of Appeals has struck down a rule that arbitrarily limited the <u>weight of an animal</u>. It should be noted, though, that the Michigan Court of Appeals has never decided whether the bylaws could contain a restriction on the weight of animals, and it is possible that a different outcome in that regard could be reached. Similarly, as outlined above, if an owner claims that an animal is necessary for assistance or emotional support, enforcement action may not be permitted if a reasonable accommodation is required under the Fair Housing Act; however, the board should consult with an attorney to determine if enforcement action should be taken.

Privacy

Technology has created privacy concerns and often results in violations of the governing documents. By way of example, many communities now pursue violations when <u>drones</u> are used despite it being prohibited in the community or when drones are used for an improper purpose. Similarly, some owners now use doorbells with cameras that are prohibited by the governing documents or that have been installed in violation of the governing documents. Finally, many people use smartphones to record their neighbors or record association meetings, even if prohibited from doing so by the governing documents. Accordingly, it is becoming more common for associations to pursue violations for these privacy-related issues.

Rental

The Michigan Condominium Act places restrictions on renting condominium units. Specifically, MCL 559.212(2) states the following:

A co-owner, including the developer, desiring to rent or lease a condominium unit shall disclose that fact in writing to the association of co-owners at least 10 days before presenting a lease or otherwise agreeing to grant possession of a condominium unit to potential lessees or occupants and, at the same time, shall supply the association of co-owners with a copy of the exact lease for its review for its compliance with the condominium documents. The co-owner or developer shall also provide the association of co-owners with a copy of the executed lease. If no lease is to be used, then the co-owner or developer shall supply the association of co-owners with the name and address of the lessees or occupants, along with the rental amount and due dates of any rental or compensation payable to a co-owner or developer, the due dates of that rental and compensation, and the term of the proposed arrangement.

Accordingly, any unit rental must be disclosed to the condominium association and any unit lease must be provided to the condominium association. If there is no written lease, then the co-owner must notify the condominium association of the name and address of the occupants, rental amount, and due dates on which rent will be paid. Many governing documents also contain rental caps that limit the number of units that may be rented at any given time. The required disclosures under MCL 559.212(2) allow a condominium association to evaluate whether a rental cap has been exceeded, among other possible violations or concerns.

A co-owner's failure to comply with MCL 559.212 is a violation of the Michigan Condominium Act and almost always a violation of the condominium bylaws, which typically contain provisions that mirror MCL 559.212(2). As such, if the association discovers that a unit is being rented and it was not notified of the rental, it should send a bylaw violation letter to the co-owner, advising them of the violation. If the co-owner still does not comply with MCL 559.212, then the association can potentially fine the co-owner or initiate court proceedings to obtain compliance.

Assuming that the renter is properly in the unit, MCL 559.212(3) requires all "tenants or non-co-owner occupants [to] comply with all of the conditions of the condominium documents of the condominium project..." If a written lease or rental agreement exists, then the rental agreement also must state that the tenant is required to comply with the condominium documents.

If a tenant or non-co-owner occupant violates the condominium documents, then MCL 559.212(4) allows for the condominium association to take the following action:

- The association of co-owners shall notify the co-owner by certified mail, advising of the alleged violation by the tenant. The co-owner shall have 15 days after receipt of the notice to investigate and correct the alleged breach by the tenant or advise the association of co-owners that a violation has not occurred.

- If after 15 days the association of co-owners believes that the alleged breach is not cured or may be repeated, it may institute on its behalf or derivatively by the co-owners on behalf of the association of co-owners, if it is under the control of the developer, an action for both eviction against the tenant or non-co-owner occupant and, simultaneously, for money damages against the co-owner and tenant or non-co-owner occupant for breach of the conditions of the condominium documents. The relief provided for in this section may be by summary proceeding. The association of co-owners may hold both the tenant and the co-owner liable for any damages to the general common elements caused by the co-owner or tenant in connection with the condominium unit or condominium project.

Accordingly, MCL 559.212(4) allows for the condominium association to pursue eviction proceedings as well as a claim for monetary damages against a tenant who violates the condominium documents. The condominium association also has traditional remedies for collecting fines, injunctive relief, or monetary damages from a co-owner for allowing a violation of the condominium documents to occur, as stated in MCL 559.206. In the context of homeowners associations, rental restrictions are entirely based on the governing documents.

Short-Term Rentals

Short-term rentals represent one of the most prevalent issues that community associations face today. To curb this problem, most governing documents contain restrictions on rentals, including a restriction that requires a minimum rental term. For situations where the governing documents do not contain a minimum rental term, the Michigan Court of Appeals has issued several opinions demonstrating that short-term rentals may be prohibited based upon certain types of restrictions. Examples of restrictions that may be used to curtail short-term rentals include the following:

- A restriction limiting the use of a lot or unit to <u>residential use</u>. A restriction that requires each lot to be used as a <u>single family private residence</u>, even if "leasing" is permitted.

- A restriction that bans a business use or otherwise limits the <u>commercial use</u> of a lot or unit.

- A restriction on renting, which often includes the following: (1) a rental cap limiting the number of rentals, (2) a minimum rental period, or (3) a requirement that the association be notified of any rentals.

- A restriction that bans activities that cause nuisance or annoyance.

- A restriction that requires compliance with local ordinances if the local zoning ordinance contains a ban on short-term rentals or other rental requirements.

In some cases, community associations will not have express restrictions related to short-term rentals. Even in the absence of express restrictions, Michigan courts have identified circumstances in which short-term rentals may still be banned based on the zoning ordinance. The Michigan Court of Appeals has recognized that a private citizen may bring an action to abate a nuisance arising from a violation of the zoning ordinance if that citizen can demonstrate damages that are unique to them and different from the general public. In applying this principle to short-term rentals, the Michigan Court of Appeals held that property owners could enforce a zoning ordinance against another property engaged in short-term rentals that created a nuisance on a lake.

Signs, Flags, and Holiday Decorations

Many governing documents contain restrictions on the types of signs, advertisements, flags, or holiday decorations that are permitted within a community. It is not uncommon for an owner who does not read the restrictions to put up holiday decorations at inappropriate times (or leave them up too long) or display garden flags, statutes, or other lawn ornaments that are prohibited by the governing documents. It is important to note, though, that a community association cannot restrict an owner from displaying am American flag that is no larger than 3' x 5' under the Freedom to Display the American Flag Act of 2005, 4 USC § 5 and MCL 559.156a of the Michigan Condominium Act.

If the board does not enforce the governing documents on what may seem to be smaller matters, this inaction often leads to widespread violations. Accordingly, it is important that the board take enforcement action on all violations as soon as possible. If an owner violates these aforementioned restrictions, an association reserves the right to impose fines or pursue injunctive relief.

Unauthorized Changes to Common Elements

One of the most common bylaw violations in a condominium project is a co-owner modifying the common elements without prior authorization of the board of directors. MCL 559.147(1) states the following in pertinent part regarding a co-owner modifying the general common elements:

> Subject to the prohibitions and restrictions in the condominium documents, a co-owner may make improvements or alterations within a condominium unit that do not impair the structural integrity of a structure or otherwise lessen the support of a portion of the condominium project. Except as provided in section 47a, a co-owner shall not do anything which would change the exterior appearance of a condominium unit or of any other portion of the condominium project except to the extent and subject to the conditions as the condominium documents may specify.

MCL 559.147(1) generally prohibits a unilateral alteration to the general common elements without permission of the condominium association and typically limits co-owner alterations to their unit (subject to the terms of the condominium documents). The only exceptions typically include the following:

- The master deed or condominium bylaws expressly allow a co-owner to alter the common elements without the board's permission

- The removal of all or part of an intervening partition or creation of doorways or other apertures therein, notwithstanding that the partition may in whole or in part be a common element, so long as a portion of any bearing wall or bearing column is not weakened or removed and a portion of any common element other than that partition is not damaged, destroyed, or endangered by a co-owner that owns adjoining units

- An improvement or modification for a disability-related need that has not been responded to within 60 days as required by MCL 559.147a

Almost all condominium documents prohibit a co-owner from making unilateral modifications to the common elements. This implies that, as seen in most cases, a co-owner will violate the Michigan Condominium Act and condominium documents by making a unilateral modification to the general common elements, unless one of the above limited exceptions applies. Accordingly, a condominium association should take enforcement action and obtain an injunction to remove any unauthorized modifications; however, if the board would have approved the modification if approval were sought in the first place, entering into a written modification agreement after the fact may be another way to resolve a dispute.

Unauthorized Changes to Condominium Units or Lots

One of the most common bylaw violations involves an owner making modifications to their site condominium unit or a home in a platted subdivision without first obtaining permission from the community association. While these types of bylaw violations can occur in attached condominiums, owners in site condominiums and communities that are composed of single-family homes more frequently tend to adopt a mindset that they can modify their home however they see fit. In most cases, though, the condominium documents or declaration will still contain restrictions on what can be done to a home or require that changes to the exterior of a home be approved by a homeowners association.

One of the most common examples of an unauthorized exterior modification is the installation of a fence. In _Dearborn Hills Civic Ass'n, Inc v Merhi, unpublished per curiam opinion of the Court of Appeals, issued Apr 28, 2022 (Docket No. 354905)_, the Michigan

Court of Appeals dealt with a situation in which an owner argued that they could install a fence without permission from the homeowners association. The owners attempted to argue that they lacked knowledge of the recorded restrictive covenants, they had no obligation to submit plans for approval that were required by the restrictive covenants if they completed the fence before the homeowners association obtained an injunction, and their violation of the restrictive covenants was a minor technical violation that the homeowners association could not enforce. The Court of Appeals rejected each of these arguments and held that the homeowners association was entitled to an injunction to have the fence removed. Accordingly, while owners will raise a variety of defenses, Michigan courts will often enforce the plain language of the declaration and require permission as opposed to granting forgiveness when an owner makes changes to the exterior of their home in violation of the restrictive covenants.

Another prime example of an unauthorized exterior modification is the installation of an auxiliary building, detached garage, in-law suite, outbuilding, pool house, or shed. In some instances, the governing documents will prohibit accessory buildings all together. By way of example, in _Oakwood Meadows Homeowners Ass'n v Urban, unpublished per curiam opinion of the Court of Appeals, issued June 26, 2014 (Docket No. 316193)_, the Michigan Court of Appeals held that the construction of a pump house to protect a pool pump and heater violated a restrictive covenant that prohibited "outbuildings, sheds, detached garages of the like" from being "erected, placed or permitted to remain upon any lot." Similarly, in _Newberry Estates Homeowners Ass'n v Cook, unpublished per curiam opinion of the Court of Appeals, issued Mar 15, 2011 (Docket No. 295468)_, the homeowners association's declaration prohibited any building from being erected other than a single-family dwelling with an attached garage but made an exception for accessory structures that were less than 200 square feet. After the association granted approval to install a shed, the owner exceeded the permission granted by the homeowners association and constructed a shed that violated the restrictive covenants. Accordingly, the court ordered that the shed be removed.

While fences and accessory buildings are the most common types of exterior violations, other examples of exterior violations relate to painting homes, installing new shingles, installing new siding, installing basketball or tennis courts, or putting in a new a new pool. Accordingly, community associations should be consistent in enforcing bylaw violations related to the exterior appearance of a home because it is necessary to preserve the aesthetics of the community.

Remedies for Enforcing the Governing Documents

The Michigan Condominium Act, specifically MCL 559.206, provides the following remedies for violations of the condominium documents:

A default by a co-owner shall entitle the association of co-owners to the following relief:

(a) Failure to comply with any of the terms or provisions of the condominium documents shall be grounds for relief, which may include without limitations, an action to recover sums due for damages, injunctive relief, foreclosure of lien if default in payment of assessment, or any combination thereof.

(b) In a proceeding arising because of an alleged default by a co-owner, the association of co-owners or the co-owner, if successful, shall recover the costs of the proceeding and reasonable attorney fees, as determined by the court, to the extent the condominium documents expressly so provide.

(c) Such other reasonable remedies the condominium documents may provide including but without limitation the levying of fines against co-owners after notice and hearing thereon and the imposition of late charges for nonpayment of assessments as provided in the condominium bylaws or rules and regulations of the condominium.

In the context of homeowners associations, the remedies for violating the governing documents are typically limited to pursuing a claim for breach of covenant to obtain compliance with the declaration, unless the governing documents provide additional remedies. Common remedies for bylaw violations are as follows:

- **Fines**. MCL 559.206 only permits a condominium association to impose fines after notice and a hearing on the fine. The governing documents of most community associations permit an association to levy fines and typically require the association to provide a warning letter prior to imposing a fine. If the owner does not stop violating the governing documents, then typically the community association must provide an additional notice and hold a hearing for the board to decide whether to levy a fine against the owner. A fine may still be levied against the owner even if they do not show up for the hearing. In most cases, the governing documents provide an escalating fine schedule and the board must comply with these schedules when imposing fines. While fines can be effective tools for managing some violations, in many cases they may not be effective in remedying issues such as commercial use of a unit, unauthorized construction, marijuana use, pets, smoking, or rentals. In these types of situations, many owners may simply pay the fine and continue the violation.

- **Injunctive Relief**. MCL 559.165 of the Michigan Condominium Act requires that every owner "... comply with the master deed, bylaws, and rules and regulations of the condominium project…" Similarly, in the context of a homeowners association, in *Terrien v Zwit*, 467 Mich 56; 648 NW2d 602 (2002), the Michigan Supreme Court has held as follows:

> … [A] breach of a covenant, no matter how minor and no matter how *de minimis* the damages, can be the subject of enforcement…If the construction of the instrument be clear and the breach clear, then it is not a question of damage, but the mere circumstance of the breach of the covenant affords sufficient ground for the Court to interfere by injunction.

Accordingly, in most cases, an injunction is the most effective way of enforcing the governing documents. An injunction is a form of relief in which a court either compels somebody to do something or forbids them from doing something. By way of example, in *Sgriccia v Welsh*, unpublished per curiam opinion of the Court of Appeals, issued Mar 24, 2022 (Docket No. 355074), the Michigan Court of Appeals ordered a homeowner who constructed a portion of their home in violation of the restrictive covenants to demolish part of the home to comply with the restrictive covenants. While the results of an injunction may seem harsh in some cases, Michigan courts have demonstrated that the freedom to contract and enforcing restrictive covenants as written is more important than the perceived fairness of the result of enforcing a restrictive covenant.

- **Money Damages**. While injunctive relief is the most common way in which governing documents are enforced, a community association may also pursue a claim for monetary damages caused by a violation of the governing documents. By way of example, if an owner damages the common elements and the association incurs the costs for repairing those damages, then the association may pursue a claim against the owner to recover the monetary damages. In some cases, the governing documents allow the association to assess the monetary damages to a unit or lot, place a lien on the property, and foreclose on the lien if the monetary damages are not paid.

• **Attorney's Fees and Costs**. As indicated in MCL 559.206, a condominium association will be entitled to recover reasonable attorney's fees and costs in a case involving a violation of the governing documents if the condominium documents expressly so provide. The governing documents for many homeowners associations also permit the recovery of attorney's fees and costs for a violation of the declaration. Accordingly, while many disputes require each party to pay their own legal fees, community associations have a distinct advantage in enforcing the governing documents because they often can recover their attorney's fees and costs if they prevail. The Michigan Court of Appeals also has ruled that a community association may be able to recover attorney's fees for successfully defending claims brought by an owner if it involves the enforcement of the governing documents.

In _Highfield Beach at Lake Michigan v Sanderson_, 331 Mich App 636, 641; 954 NW2d 231 (2020), the Michigan Court of Appeals held that an association was allowed to recover attorney's fees and costs as follows:

Giving the language of this unambiguous bylaw its plain and ordinary meaning, we hold that the bylaw entitled HBLM to an award of attorney fees and costs associated with defending against Sanderson's counterclaim. The proceeding arose because of Sanderson's alleged default, which has now been established, and the counterclaim was part of and encompassed by the "proceeding."

Furthermore, assuming for the sake of argument that the counterclaim must be viewed as its own "proceeding" apart from the complaint for purposes of the bylaw, the counterclaim for breach of contract still constituted a proceeding arising because of an alleged default. Sanderson only filed the counterclaim because he was accused of a default for violating the amended bylaw restricting rentals—without the default there would have been no responsive counterclaim. Indeed, the breach of contract counterclaim sought money damages on the possibility that Sanderson would not be permitted to use his property for short-term rentals because of the amended bylaw. Accordingly, the trial court did not err by awarding HBLM attorney fees and costs incurred in defending against the counterclaim.

Accordingly, given that community association board members must enforce the governing documents as written and most associations can recover attorney's fees and costs for prevailing in an action related to the enforcement of governing documents, community associations must be diligent in pursuing enforcement remedies.

Chapter 5

------- ⚹ -------

Collections

The sole source of income for most community associations comes from assessment payments. Income from assessments is used to provide essential services and to fund association operations. If an owner fails to pay assessments, all the other owners suffer because they must shoulder the burden of the association's operational costs. With that in mind, in this chapter, we will discuss the particulars of collections, how a community association can streamline the collection process, and what to do in situations when an owner becomes delinquent.

Can Co-Owners Withhold Assessment Payments?

If a co-owner is unhappy with their condominium association, they may threaten to withhold their assessments. Common reasons that owners attempt to withhold assessment payments include, but are not limited to, the following:

- A condominium unit has sustained damage and the co-owner believes the condominium association has not responded as quickly or thoroughly as it should have.

99

- A co-owner is unhappy with the repairs made to their unit.

- A co-owner is dissatisfied with some aspect of how the condominium association is operating, such as accounting practices or the board's financial decisions.

- A co-owner is not receiving the services that they expected.

- A co-owner is dissatisfied with the board for political reasons.

None of these reasons, though, gives a co-owner the right to withhold assessment payments. While Michigan law permits tenants to withhold payment if repairs are not timely made, this concept does not apply to condominium associations. Specifically, MCL 559.239 of the Michigan Condominium Act states that "[a] co-owner may not assert in an answer, or set off to a complaint brought by the association for non-payment of assessments the fact that the association of co-owners or its agents have not provided the services or management to a co-owner(s)."

Accordingly, co-owners who withhold payments should be made aware that they cannot withhold assessment payments under Michigan law and that they may incur late fees, interest, attorney's fees, and costs and potentially face foreclosure if they do not pay assessments in a timely manner.

All Community Associations Should Have a Collection Policy

All community associations should adopt a collection policy as part of their rules and regulations to protect a community association from issues with delinquent payments and other cash flow problems. With a clear collection policy, owners will know what is expected of them, when they need to pay, and what kinds of penalties they will incur if they do not pay. A collection policy is also important to avoid claims of selective enforcement and ensure that all owners are treated the same in the collection process. A typical collection policy should identify the following:

- The due date for assessments and the date that interest or late fees will begin to accrue.

- The time period during which the association or management company will send a follow-up letter for any missed payments.

- The time period for turning over delinquent assessments to legal counsel.

- Whether legal counsel will send an additional demand letter to a delinquent owner.

- Whether assessments will be accelerated, if permitted by the governing documents.

- Whether a rent diversion letter will be sent to the tenant of a condominium unit, as permitted by MCL 559.212.

- How payments will be applied to delinquent accounts, i.e., will they first be applied to attorney's fees, costs, late fees, or interest, before applying payments to outstanding assessments.

- The time period during which a lien will be recorded on the property if the default remains ongoing.

- The time period during which foreclosure will be commenced or a complaint will be filed in court if the co-owner's account remains delinquent.

Most collection policies also provide the board with discretion to enter into payment plans. In exercising this discretion, the board should ensure that a delinquent owner provides evidence that they are suffering from a financial hardship that requires a payment plan.

If a community association takes an inflexible position with delinquent owners from the outset, such an action may force the owner to declare bankruptcy, which can complicate matters; however, accepting a payment plan does not mean that a community association should accept less than the total amount of assessments owed. While providing a "discount" may seem like a neighborly thing to do, in reality, it only shifts the financial burden onto the other owners. Accordingly, while the Michigan Court of Appeals has held that board has the authority to enter into a settlement agreement and <u>temporarily waive the association's ability to collect assessments</u>, the court also noted that doing so would create a deficit in the association's annual budget. If the board of directors would like to compromise with a delinquent co-owner, even though it is under no obligation to do so, it should first consider waiving late fees or interest because the waiver of these items does not create a budget deficit for the association.

How Should Your Condominium Association Handle Foreclosures?

In Michigan, condominium associations have a statutory lien for unpaid assessments under the Michigan Condominium Act. In contrast, a homeowners association only has the authority to place a lien, and foreclose, if permitted to do so by the governing documents. Accordingly, community associations should ensure that they have the right to place and foreclose a lien under the governing documents because not all homeowners associations are able to do so. If a homeowners association does not have the right to place or foreclose a lien, its remedy will be limited to obtaining a money judgment to collect unpaid assessments, as discussed below.

Judicial foreclosure

Judicial foreclosure starts when the community association files a lawsuit against the delinquent owner to foreclose on its assessment lien. The association can request a monetary judgment against the owner in addition to a judgment of foreclosure. If the owner does not respond to the community association's lawsuit, then the association may seek a default judgment. If granted, the default judgment would give the association the relief it requested in the complaint, which is typically the monetary judgment or judgment of foreclosure. If the co-owner disputes the amount owed, then the court will determine the amount owed.

Whether the judgment is obtained via default, summary disposition, or after trial, the association must wait for 21 days before taking action to enforce or collect a money judgment. Additionally, the association cannot seek to have the property sold until at least six months have passed after the filing of the lawsuit. If the association also obtains a judgment allowing it to foreclose on the property, the association must conduct a sheriff's sale, which ordinarily takes place at the circuit county courthouse. All members of the public, including the association, may bid on the property at the sheriff's sale. In most circumstances, the association enters a full credit bid (i.e., a bid in the amount of the judgment plus any additional expenses) as the opening bid for the property. If the property is sold for a price greater than the opening bid amount, then the owner is entitled to receive the surplus after the association is paid what it is owed.

A successful purchaser will receive a sheriff's deed that will be recorded in the register of deeds. The redemption period, which is the time period given to borrowers in foreclosure during which they can buy back or "redeem" their property after foreclosure, begins to run from the date the sheriff's deed is recorded. The redemption period is six months from the date of the sheriff's sale, unless the property is deemed abandoned, in which case the redemption period expires one month from the date of sale.

From a practical standpoint, a major advantage of judicial foreclosures is that the association can seek a monetary judgment in addition to a judgment of foreclosure. Thus, if the owner is uncollectable, then the association can seek to foreclose on the property and take possession, and the property can be sold to a third party or leased out to allow the association to recover its costs.

Moreover, if the owner is collectible and there is no equity in the property, then the association can seek to recover on the monetary judgment and garnish wages or bank accounts of the delinquent owner. Another advantage of judicial foreclosures is that the association may seek to have a receiver appointed to collect rent during the litigation if there is a tenant in the property. For these reasons, judicial foreclosures provide an association with more flexibility in pursuing delinquent owners; however, as will be discussed below, judicial foreclosure is often more time consuming and expensive, so many associations prefer to foreclose by advertisement.

Foreclosure by Advertisement

Foreclosure by advertisement allows a community association to foreclose its lien and sell the property without going to court. While a condominium association has a statutory lien that arises as a matter of law, MCL 559.208(3) requires a condominium association to send notice of a condominium lien to a delinquent co-owner by first-class mail, addressed to the last known address of the co-owner, at least 10 days before foreclosing; however, the Michigan Court of Appeals has held that <u>actual notice</u> of the lien is not required to be provided by a condominium association to a co-owner in order to foreclose, such as if the co-owner does not receive the notice at their last known address.

After a condominium association serves its lien under MCL 559.208, the association is only required to publish a notice in the local newspaper if it desires to foreclose by advertisement, as opposed to commencing a court proceeding. The statute governing foreclosure by advertisement is <u>MCL 600.3201</u>, et seq., which requires a notice of foreclosure to be published at least once per week for four consecutive weeks with a newspaper published in the county where the property is located.

The association is also required to post a copy of the notice in a conspicuous place on the property, which is usually the front door. Many governing documents include an additional requirement that the association notify the co-owner that it will be pursuing foreclosure by advertisement and advise them that they are permitted to request a judicial hearing by bringing suit against the association.

If the owner fails to pay the amount stated in the notice, then a sale is scheduled and the county sheriff conducts the sale in the same manner as a judicial foreclosure. Like a judicial foreclosure, the owner who has defaulted on their assessments has the right to redeem the property after foreclosure. As with a judicial foreclosure, the redemption period in a foreclosure by advertisement is six months, unless the property is deemed abandoned, in which case the redemption period is one month.

The main advantage of foreclosing by advertisement is that the process is much quicker than a judicial foreclosure. When considering the time to file the lawsuit, serve the lawsuit, have the lawsuit answered, file a motion, and obtain a judgment, there is typically a minimum of seven to eight months before the association can foreclose if it decides to pursue judicial foreclosure. Judicial foreclosures are more complex and expensive than foreclosure by advertisement as well.

In addition, foreclosure by advertisement only requires publishing and posting of the foreclosure notice. Accordingly, an owner cannot evade service to avoid a foreclosure by advertisement. Finally, foreclosure by advertisement does not give the owner the right to raise a defense or challenge the foreclosure or the balance owed unless they file a lawsuit in court, putting the financial burden of initiating litigation on the owner instead of the association. Foreclosure by advertisement forces an owner to pay off the balance in full or risk losing their home in a short period of time and can be an extremely valuable tool for associations to compel payment.

Whether the foreclosure is conducted judicially or by advertisement, if the association purchases the property at the foreclosure sale and the property is subject to a senior lien, such as a first mortgage or a state or federal tax lien, then the association only owns the property and is entitled to lease the property until the senior lienholder forecloses its lien, at which time the association's interest is terminated.

Lien Priority

It is important for an association to record liens for unpaid association assessments to protect its lien priority. In the context of condominiums, MCL 559.208(1) states the following regarding lien priority:

> Sums assessed to a co-owner by the association of co-owners that are unpaid together with interest on such sums, collection and late charges, advances made by the association of co-owners for taxes or other liens to protect its lien, attorney fees, and fines in accordance with the condominium documents, constitute a lien upon the unit or units in the project owned by the co-owner at the time of the assessment before other liens except tax liens on the condominium unit in favor of any state or federal taxing authority and sums unpaid on a first mortgage of record, except that past due assessments that are evidenced by a

notice of lien recorded as set forth in subsection (3) have priority over a first mortgage recorded subsequent to the recording of the notice of lien.

At least one federal court, though, has ruled that a condominium lien that was recorded before a federal tax lien may take priority over the federal lien based on federal law. Similarly, it is important to record a lien on a unit even if there is no mortgage because the condominium lien has priority over a first mortgage of record that is recorded after the condominium lien was recorded; however, a condominium association lien may not be protected if the condominium association accepts a deed in lieu of foreclosure and allows junior liens to remain on the property. In the context of a homeowners association, the declaration may determine the association's lien priority; however, generally speaking, Michigan is a race-notice state, meaning that the first recorded interest takes priority. Specifically, MCL 565.29 states that "[e]very conveyance of real estate within the state hereafter made, which shall not be recorded as provided in this chapter, shall be void as against any subsequent purchaser in good faith and for a valuable consideration, of the same real estate or any portion thereof, whose conveyance shall be first duly recorded."

While there may be certain statutory exceptions to this general rule, such as for state or federal taxes, it is especially important for a homeowners association to record liens, if permitted to do so by its governing documents, in a timely manner because they do not have the same statutory priority granted to condominium associations.

When Is a Bank or Other Mortgage Lender Obligated to Pay Assessments After a Foreclosure?

If a co-owner's mortgage lender forecloses on them, is the lender then obligated to pay the co-owner's assessments? Yes and no. The lender will not be responsible for any delinquent assessment payments *prior* to the time the bank foreclosed on the unit. After the bank forecloses, they will be responsible for any assessments due from the date of the sheriff's sale going forward.

What Happens When an Owner Declares Bankruptcy?

Declaring bankruptcy is a means to resolve debt, either through asset liquidation or debt consolidation. If an owner files for bankruptcy, they will file under either Chapter 7 or Chapter 13. In Chapter 7 bankruptcy, the debtor has a low-income threshold and largely unsecured debt, and their non-exempt assets will be sold to pay their debts back to their creditors (including your association). Unfortunately, in most cases, there is not enough money collected from these sales to pay off debtors and the association may not recoup most, or any, of the assessments owed.

In a Chapter 13 bankruptcy, the debtor commits to a repayment plan of some or all of their debt over a period of three to five years; however, there is no guarantee that the association's assessments will be among the debts paid off in full and it may not see any repayment at all.

In Chapter 7 bankruptcy, the owner will typically surrender their unit and then be granted a discharge order by the bankruptcy court. A discharge order prohibits a community association from attempting to collect assessments accruing prior to the bankruptcy filing; however, the owner will be responsible for assessments that accrued after the bankruptcy was filed if they have an ownership interest in the unit. If the owner intends to keep the unit, then they will be responsible for paying back all assessments owed to the condominium association.

In Chapter 13 cases, the owner may either surrender or keep the unit. If the owner surrenders the unit and is granted a discharge, then the association will not be able to collect pre-bankruptcy filing assessments, but it may collect payment on delinquent assessments accruing during the bankruptcy term. If the owner is allowed to keep their unit, then they will be responsible for paying both pre-bankruptcy and post-bankruptcy assessments.

You can protect your association by ensuring all liens are filed in a timely manner when the owner becomes delinquent. In most cases, this will ensure that the association is not significantly impacted by the owner's bankruptcy.

This should help you better understand how to collect assessments and how to ensure that your community association is paid what it needs to operate smoothly and ensure a successful community experience for your members; however, you should consult with a qualified community association attorney to handle complicated collection issues if your initial collection efforts are unsuccessful.

Chapter 6

⊼

Amending the Governing Documents

Community associations must regularly review their governing documents to ensure smooth operations and avoid exposure to litigation. This chapter will identify common reasons why a community association must update its governing documents.

Do Your Articles of Incorporation Need to Be Updated?

When did your community association last update its articles of incorporation? Major changes were made to the Michigan Nonprofit Corporation Act in 2008 and 2015, and if your articles of incorporation were drafted prior to these dates, they may be <u>outdated</u>. Similarly, COVID-19 changed the way that many associations operate.

Accordingly, a community association should review its articles of incorporation to determine if they address the following issues:

Assumption of Director and Officer Liability

The articles of incorporation should indicate whether the association will assume the liability of a volunteer director, volunteer officer, or other volunteer, such as a committee member. An association may assume the liability of a volunteer under the Michigan Nonprofit Corporation Act, specifically MCL 450.2209, in the following circumstances:

- The volunteer was acting, or reasonably believed they were acting, within the scope of their authority.

- The volunteer was acting in good faith.

- The volunteer's conduct did not amount to gross negligence or willful and wanton misconduct.

- The volunteer's conduct was not an intentional tort.

- The volunteer's conduct was not a tort arising out of the ownership, maintenance, or use of a motor vehicle for which tort liability may be imposed, as provided in Section 3135 of the Insurance Code of 1956, Act 218 of the Public Acts of 1956, MCL 500.3135, et seq.

It is also important to understand that the above liability protections only apply to **volunteers**. If a director or officer receives payment for their services in excess of any reimbursements, they likely would not be entitled to have the association assume liability on their behalf. While it is not common, some governing documents permit directors and officers to be compensated. Accordingly, given that any compensation provided in the governing documents is nominal, we typically recommend that directors and officers maintain their volunteer status for liability purposes.

Limitation of Director and Officer Liability

The articles of incorporation are important because they also determine the standard of liability for directors and volunteer officers. The articles of incorporation may contain a provision that eliminates a director's or volunteer officer's liability to the association or its members for **money damages**, except for the following types of claims:

- A financial benefit received by a director or volunteer officer to which they were not entitled.

- Harm that was intentionally inflicted on the association or its members.

- The receipt of an unlawful distribution made by the association.

- An intentional criminal act.

- An award of attorney's fees and costs to a successful plaintiff in a derivative action filed against a director or officer.

While some owners may object to amending the articles of incorporation to reduce director liability, these types of amendments have various benefits that impact all owners, such as:

- Preventing lawsuits that deter volunteer directors and officers from serving on the board of directors.

- Reducing potential claims against board members that may increase the costs of the directors and officers insurance for the condominium and homeowners association in the future.

- Reducing the possibility that the condominium or homeowners association will incur unforeseen expenses to indemnify an officer or director for a lawsuit that is not covered by directors and officers insurance.

- Providing additional defenses that may reduce the length and expense of a lawsuit.

Accordingly, while some members may think that eliminating director and officer liability only benefits the individuals serving on the board, there are benefits to the entire community for setting a high threshold to filing a lawsuit against the directors and officers of a homeowners association.

Emergency Powers

The articles of incorporation also identify the powers of a community association. As a result of the COVID-19 pandemic and the Surfside condominium collapse, many community associations have updated their articles of incorporation to include emergency powers.

Examples of emergency powers that may be included in the articles of incorporation include authority for the board of directors to do the following:

- To take any action necessary to implement any order or guidance of a governmental entity, even if it conflicts with the governing documents.

- To determine that any portion of the community is unavailable for entry, occupancy, or use or is limited in occupancy or use in the event of an emergency.

- To temporarily delay or suspend the enforcement of any provision of the governing documents due to an emergency.

- To adjourn any association meeting to a later date to the extent permitted by law, even if such a meeting is required to be held under the governing documents.

Voting

The amendments to the Michigan Nonprofit Corporation Act expanded the manner in which community associations can hold elections and members can participate in association meetings. Specifically, unless prohibited by the governing documents, members may now participate in membership meetings via electronic means or via telephone as long as two-way communication is permitted. Accordingly, the articles of incorporation should be reviewed to ensure that they do not prevent electronic or telephonic participation in meetings. Similarly, instead of requiring members to physically appear at a meeting to place their votes, they can now vote through electronic transmission or at a designated polling place, if such provisions are included in the governing documents. Finally, if the articles of incorporation do not permit an action without meeting (a method of voting in which the owners can vote by ballot outside of a meeting), the articles of incorporation should be amended to permit this type of voting. In addition to making it easier for owners to vote, the above provisions are also useful in establishing quorum and making sure that votes are passed.

Accordingly, if your community association has not recently amended its articles of incorporation, it is likely time that you do so to account for changes in the law and technology. Generally speaking, a majority of a quorum at a meeting of the association can vote to amend the articles of incorporation under the Michigan Nonprofit Corporation Act, unless the articles of incorporation contain a heightened approval requirement. As a result, the articles of incorporation are typically easier to update than other governing documents that may require approval of 2/3 of the owners.

When Should You Amend Your Master Deed, Condominium Bylaws, or Declaration?

The foundation for properly operating any community association is having a good set of governing documents. In many cases, disputes arise when the governing documents are missing provisions required by law, Accordingly, it is a good idea to have a community association attorney review the governing documents to ensure that they comply with applicable statutes. In our firm, we have developed a condominium report card to check for legal compliance issues, which include the items discussed in this chapter.

- **The master deed and condominium bylaws do not contain provisions required by the Michigan Condominium Act.** The Michigan Condominium Act and administrative rules require that various provisions be contained in the condominium documents. In some cases, the developer forgets to include <u>mandatory</u> provisions in the condominium documents. Accordingly, a condominium association should update their condominium documents to ensure that they comply with the Michigan Condominium Act and administrative rules. Examples of required provisions in condominium documents include:

1. The name and location of the condominium.

2. The name of the condominium association.

3. Identifying whether the condominium association is a nonprofit corporation, partnership, or unincorporated association.

4. A limitation on membership in the condominium association to co-owners and a requirement that each co-owner be a member of the association.

5. A statement that expenditures affecting the administration of the condominium project include costs incurred in the satisfaction of any liability arising within, caused by, or connected with the common elements or the administration of the condominium project, and that receipts affecting the administration of the condominium project shall include all sums received as the proceeds of, or pursuant to, a policy of insurance securing the interest of the co-owners against liabilities or losses arising within, caused by, or connected with the common elements or the administration of the condominium project.

6. Provisions that require the association to carry insurance for fire and extended coverage, vandalism, and malicious mischief and, if applicable, liability and workers' disability compensation pertinent to the ownership, use, and maintenance of the premises and that all premiums for insurance carried by the association shall be an expense of administration.

7. A requirement that the condominium keep the books and records of the association, including current copies of the governing documents, and that the books and records will be available for inspection.

8. A requirement that the association prepare and distribute to each owner a financial statement on an annual basis.

9. A requirement that the association have its books and records audited or reviewed on an annual basis by a CPA as a cost of administration unless the association opts out.

10. A requirement that each co-owner who mortgages their unit must notify the association of the name and address of the mortgagee and that the association shall keep a book of records that contains all the mortgagee information.

11. The method by which assessments are calculated and a requirement that the board of directors establish an annual budget.

12. The procedures to be followed when a co-owner fails to pay assessments.

13. A requirement that the association establish a reserve fund for major repairs and replacement, along with following statement: "The minimum standard required by this section may prove to be inadequate for a particular project. The association of co-owners should carefully analyze their condominium project to determine if a greater amount should be set aside, or if additional reserve funds should be established for other purposes."

14. A statement that a co-owner desiring to rent a unit must disclose that fact to the association at least 10 days before

presenting a lease or agreeing to grant possession to a potential lessee or other occupant.

15. A statement that all present and future co-owners, tenants, and any other persons or occupants using the facilities of the project in any manner are subject to and shall comply with the Michigan Condominium Act and condominium documents.

16. A statement that provides that the arbitration of disputes, claims, and grievances arising out of or relating to the interpretation of the application of the condominium documents or arising out of disputes among or between co-owners shall be submitted to arbitration and that the parties to the dispute, claim, or grievance shall accept the arbitrator's decision as final and binding, upon the election and written consent of the parties to the disputes, claims, or grievances and upon written notice to the association (though this requirement does not apply to those condominiums created prior to the date of the amendatory act which added the requirement).

17. An indemnification clause for the members of the board that excludes indemnification for willful and wanton misconduct and for gross negligence.

18. A statement that describes what happens in the event of partial or complete destruction of the building(s) in the project.

- **The developer's attorney wrote the master deed, bylaws, or declaration.** In most cases, the developer's attorney drafts the master deed and condominium bylaws or declaration to protect the developer and not the interests of the owners and the community association.

- **The master deed, bylaws, or declaration contain contra-dictory, incomplete, or unclear provisions.** Your governing documents should be written in clear, plain language. If an association's governing documents have provisions that are incomplete, contradictory, or unclear in any way, they should be amended to avoid disputes between the association and the owners.

- **The master deed, bylaws, or declaration do not have appropriate liability disclaimers.** While a community association's general liability insurance policy will cover many things, a community association needs to have appropriate documents to fill in the gaps for items that typically are not covered. Examples of items that the association should disclaim liability for in the governing documents are damage resulting from criminal acts of third parties, damage from COVID-19 or other viruses, incidental damage caused by the common elements or common areas that may be covered under the owner's insurance policy, or acts of God that are beyond the association's control.

- **Insurance and maintenance responsibilities do not align.** It is important that the governing documents in a community association are clear on the insurance obligations of the association and the owners. Many older governing documents are unclear on insurance coverage or create overlapping insurance responsibilities, which may lead to disputes. Accordingly, we recommend that unclear governing documents be updated to include a primary carrier provision and to indicate that the party responsible for the repair of a common element or unit will have the primary insurance obligation on this area as well. If the insurance provisions in governing documents are not clear, it will typically lead to disputes between the condominium association, co-owner, and their respective insurance adjusters and slow down the adjustment of insurance claims.

119

Red Flags That Your Governing Documents May Be Outdated

Think of your governing documents like a car. If you do not perform regular maintenance, such as changing the oil, the car will eventually become non-functional. Many community associations put off updating their master deed, bylaws, or declaration because they fear the cost, but failing to update these governing documents may make it difficult to operate your community association, or even worse, result in expensive litigation. Common indicators that governing documents are outdated and in need of updating are:

- **The master deed and bylaws were written before 2002.** In 2001 and 2002, the Michigan legislature made significant amendments to the Michigan Condominium Act. Master deeds and condominium bylaws written before these time periods are likely outdated and in need of amendment because they do not contain these major statutory changes.

- **The governing documents do not have a rental cap or prohibit short-term rentals.** With a few exceptions, namely vacation condominium developments and condominium hotels, most condominium projects are developed with the intent that the co-owners will be owner-occupants. In the wake of the housing crash, though, investors across the country bought condominium units and other properties to rent out to tenants. As a result, we have seen a big influx of renters in condominium developments across Michigan. Too many renters can cause a number of issues for condominium associations, but a rental cap can help prevent these issues. Similarly, in the last few years we have seen the rise of vacation rental services such as Airbnb and VRBO. As a result, we have seen a rise in issues with owners, associations, and short-term renters. Savvy boards and community associations are making amendments to their governing documents to restrict or expressly prohibit short-term rentals or listing units on these types of platforms.

- **The governing documents do not contemplate electric vehicles.** By 2040, experts project at least 35% of all new vehicles will be hybrids or fully-electric vehicles. That means that over the next few years, you can expect a lot more requests from owners to install electric vehicle charging stations. If your governing documents do not contain provisions that outline requirements related to the installation of electric vehicle charging stations, it may be time for an update.

- **The governing documents do not address social media.** Community associations are often forced to deal with individual owners creating websites or pages on social media sites, such as Facebook or Nextdoor, that appear to be sponsored by the association. In some cases, the owner may violate trademark rights of the association if they cause confusion by using items such as the association logo in creating an online presence that impersonates the association. The easiest way to prevent these types of issues is through adopting express restrictions in the governing documents or creating rules to prevent owners from misusing the association's name and likeness online.

- **The governing documents do not address Wi-Fi issues.** In some cases, you will not need to make any amendments to your governing documents concerning Wi-Fi. For example, if you do not have a Wi-Fi network available for use in common elements and if all the owners are responsible for their own Wi-Fi, you may not need an amendment; however, if you have plans for any type of community Wi-Fi network, you must address it in your governing documents to avoid issues later.

- **The governing documents do not address other technology issues.** You might think you do not need to update your governing documents because they were last updated long after the last major changes made to the Michigan Condominium Act came into effect; however, <u>drones</u>, ring doorbells, and smartphones were not widely available at easily affordable prices until recently. Similarly, many energy-efficient, money-saving home upgrades were not available on a wide scale until just a few years ago, such as solar panels or generators. Do your governing documents address the challenges and opportunities that these technological innovations present?

- **<u>The governing documents do not address marijuana.</u>** Michigan decriminalized recreational use of marijuana in 2018, but marijuana remains illegal under federal law. Accordingly, there are potential civil and criminal liability issues, as well as the potential loss of insurance coverage, if a community association permits marijuana use within their community. Therefore, community associations should ensure that they have express provisions in the governing documents that ban the use of marijuana to avoid any confusion among the owners regarding this issue.

- **<u>The governing documents do not account for the Surfside collapse.</u>** One lesson learned from the Surfside collapse is that the board of directors must be empowered to appropriately take care of the building. Unfortunately, many governing documents often place restrictions on the board's ability to adequately maintain, repair, and replace various common elements and require certain co-owner approvals that slow down or make required maintenance impossible. In other circumstances, the board may have too much discretion and may opt not to perform important tasks as cost-cutting measures. Examples of restrictions that can be <u>amended</u> to permit the board of directors to adequately care for a building include:

1. Removing overly burdensome voting requirements that prevent board members from imposing assessments or

obtaining a loan to make necessary repairs without owner approval.

2. Removing anti-lawsuit provisions from condominium documents so developers may be held accountable for construction defects.

3. Requiring a condominium association to perform regular inspections of the common elements or mandating regular reserve studies, instead of making these items optional.

4. Requiring a condominium association to have a reserve fund that is tied to a reserve study or that is in excess of the statutory minimum of 10% of the association's current annual budget.

What Is the Process for Amending a Master Deed, Condominium Bylaws, or Declaration?

In the context of condominium associations, the Michigan Condominium Act requires 2/3 of the co-owners who are eligible to vote to approve a material amendment to the master deed and condominium bylaws. As such, the co-owners must affirmatively vote to amend the master deed and condominium bylaws. Additionally, there are certain types of amendments that mortgagees can vote on. Specifically, mortgagees may vote on the following types of amendments:

• Termination of the condominium project.

• Changes to the formula or method used to determine the percentage of value of the condominium project assigned to a unit subject to the mortgagee's mortgage.

- Reallocation of responsibilities for maintenance, replacements, repairs, or decoration of a unit, its appurtenant limited common elements, or the general common elements from the association of co-owners to the unit subject to the mortgagee's mortgage.

- Elimination of a requirement for the condominium association to maintain insurance on the condominium project as a whole or condominium unit, subject to the mortgagee's mortgage.

- Reallocation of responsibility for obtaining and maintaining insurance from the association to the unit subject to the mortgagee's mortgage.

- Modification or elimination of an easement benefiting the unit subject to the mortgagee's mortgage.

- Partial or complete modification, imposition, or removal of leasing restrictions for units in the project.

- Amendments to the method or formula used to determine the percentage of value of units in the project for purposes other than voting or an amendment that alters the size or appurtenant common elements of a unit.

Please keep in mind that the mortgagee voting process is different than the co-owner voting process and it takes place after co-owner approval has been obtained. Unlike the co-owner voting process, where an affirmative vote is required, the mortgagee voting process takes place within a 90-day window. If the mortgagees do not respond to the request for a vote within the 90-day window, it counts as a vote to approve the amendment.

In contrast, the declaration of a homeowners association may be amended as a matter of contract based upon the amendment requirements in the declaration. Many homeowners association documents set certain time periods during which the governing documents can be amended. If there is no amendment provision in a declaration, <u>unanimous consent</u> of all lots will be required to amend the governing documents.

In most cases, a homeowners association will have a separate set of corporate bylaws that outlines procedures for operating the association. While many condominium associations will combine the corporate bylaws with the condominium bylaws, some older condominium associations may also have a separate set of corporate bylaws. Similar to a declaration, the corporate bylaws will typically outline an amendment process for amending the corporate bylaws.

What Types of Document Amendments Do Not Require a Co-Owner Vote?

In limited circumstances, the condominium documents can be amended without a vote of the co-owners. MCL 559.190(1) permits non-material amendments by a developer or board of directors, if specially permitted by the governing documents, and states as follows:

> The condominium documents may be amended without the consent of co-owners or mortgagees if the amendment does not materially alter or change the rights of a co-owner or mortgagee and if the condominium documents contain a reservation of the right to amend for that purpose to the developer or the association of co-owners. An amendment that does not materially change the rights of a co-owner or mortgagee includes, but is not limited

to, a modification of the types and sizes of unsold condominium units and their appurtenant limited common elements.

While there is little case law that defines what is a "material amendment" under MCL 559.190, there is at least one Michigan case that held that an amendment to the quorum requirements in the condominium bylaws constituted a non-material amendment that could be achieved by the board as opposed to a vote of the co-owners.

Moreover, other sections of the Michigan Condominium Act expressly permit certain types of amendments to the master deed without co-owner approval. By way of example, MCL 559.148 permits the board of directors of a condominium association to relocate unit boundaries without a vote. Accordingly, a co-owner may purchase two adjoining units and move the boundary between them only with board approval. MCL 559.149 permits the subdivision of units through an amendment to the master deed that is only approved by the association's board of directors. Finally, MCL 559.137 permits the board to approve an amendment to a master deed that transfers limited common elements, such as parking spaces, without co-owner approval based on an application from the co-owners desiring to transfer the limited common elements.

When in doubt as to whether an amendment to the governing documents requires owner approval, it is always a good idea to seek counsel from a qualified community association attorney. In many cases, we have seen developers, board members, or attorneys that are not familiar with community association law attempt amendments to the governing documents without appropriate approval, which leads to confusion among the members and, in some cases, expensive litigation over the validity of an amendment.

How to Properly Use Rule-Making Authority

Rules and regulations are used by the board of directors of a community association to implement the existing governing documents. In most cases, the governing documents will permit the board of directors to enact rules and regulations without a vote of the owners. In *Meadow Bridge Condo Ass'n v Bosca*, 187 Mich App 280, 282; 466 NW2d 303 (1990), the Michigan Court of Appeals held that "a rule or regulation is a tool to implement or manage existing structural law." Accordingly, rules and regulations cannot be used to amend the governing documents, but they can be used to implement the existing governing documents. When enacting rules, the board of directors should be careful and ensure that they can point to a specific provision in the governing documents that is being implemented by the rule. In *Mt Vernon Park Ass'n v Clark,* unpublished per curiam opinion of the Court of Appeals, issued Dec 29, 2015 (Docket No. 323445), the Michigan Court of Appeals invalidated a set of rules because the court indicated that an association could not create rules and regulations that were inconsistent with the master deed and condominium bylaws. Common examples of rules and regulations that boards enact are:

- Antenna and Satellite Dish Guidelines

- Architectural Control Procedures

- Bylaw Enforcement Policies

- Clubhouse Rules

- Code of Conduct for Directors

- Collection Policies

- Common Area Use Rules

- COVID-19 Protocols

- Design Guidelines

- Fine Procedures

- Meeting Rules

- Pool Rules

- Recreational Facility Rules

Chapter 7

Fair Housing

Residential community associations are required to comply with the federal Fair Housing Act, 42 USC § 3601, et seq. The Fair Housing Act protects owners and occupants in community associations from discrimination based on race, color, religion, sex, national origin, familial status, and disability. Unfortunately, the Fair Housing Act is one of the trickiest statutes for community associations to comply with because it is complicated, and it is not difficult for well-intentioned community association boards to run afoul of the statute. Accordingly, if your community association encounters a fair housing issue, it is highly recommended to consult with an attorney because each case is very fact-specific and there are many nuisances in this area of law; however, this chapter will outline some of the common fair housing issues encountered by community associations so you know when it may be appropriate to contact the association's legal counsel for help.

The Process for Fair Housing Claims

In Michigan, a fair housing claim may be initiated by an owner or occupant against a community association or its directors, officers, or management company in several different ways. First, and the most common way, is that an owner or occupant may file a claim with the Michigan Department of Civil Rights ("MDCR"). After a fair housing complaint is filed with the MDCR, a community association will receive notification of the claim and will have an opportunity to respond in writing. The MDCR will then investigate the claim to determine if it has any merit. In many cases, they will go through a conciliation process and attempt to mediate the dispute between the parties. If there is no merit to the claim, the MDCR may dismiss the matter. If a resolution cannot be reached and the MDCR believes that the claim has merit, it may pursue a formal charge and set a date for a public administrative hearing. After the hearing, the Michigan Civil Rights Commission will determine whether the findings of the hearing officer should be adopted. If either side disagrees with the decision of the Civil Rights Commission, they may file an appeal in a Michigan circuit court.

Second, a fair housing claim may be initiated by filing a fair housing complaint with the federal Department of Housing and Urban Development ("HUD"). Similar to the state process, HUD permits the community association to file a response and will commence an investigation. HUD will also attempt to mediate the dispute through the conciliation process. If there is no merit to the claim, then HUD may dismiss the matter. If HUD believes the claim has merit, it may pursue a formal charge through a federal administrative law judge or filing an action in federal court.

Third, a fair housing claim may simply be initiated by filing a complaint in either state or federal court; however, this process typically requires the owner or occupant to hire an attorney so this is the least common way for a fair housing complaint to be initiated. Filing a complaint with MDCR or HUD, on the other hand, does not require an attorney and only requires an owner or occupant to complete and submit a form. Accordingly, these are the most common ways that a fair housing complaint is initiated.

Finally, community associations should be aware that Fair Housing Act violations can potentially carry very significant penalties if a violation is established, which include the following:

- Actual damages

- Injunctive relief

- Equitable relief to make housing available

- Reasonable attorney's fees and costs

- Civil penalties, which may range from $23,011 with no prior violations to $115,054 with two or more prior violations.

- Punitive damages

Given that insurance policies vary in whether they will provide any type of coverage for Fair Housing Act violations, it is important for associations, board members, and property managers to implement policies to ensure compliance with the Fair Housing Act given the significant penalties associated with a violation.

Theories of Liability Under the Fair Housing Act

Generally, federal courts have held that a plaintiff may establish a fair housing violation if they are able to demonstrate that they suffered disparate treatment. Disparate treatment requires that a plaintiff demonstrate that they were treated differently as a result of their race, color, religion, sex, national origin, familial status, and disability and that a community association also had a discriminatory intent or motive for their actions or inactions. In most cases, community association board members and property managers understand that they should not intentionally do something that would discriminate based on a protected class; however, associations and management companies need to be aware that a plaintiff could also potentially demonstrate a violation of the Fair Housing Act based on a theory of disparate impact. Specifically, the United States Supreme Court has held that a Fair Housing Act violation may be established as follows:

> In contrast to a disparate-treatment case, where a "plaintiff must establish that the defendant had a discriminatory intent or motive," a plaintiff bringing a disparate-impact claim challenges practices that have a "disproportionately adverse effect on minorities" and are otherwise unjustified by a legitimate rationale.

Texas Dep't of Hous & Cmty Affairs v Inclusive Communities Project, Inc, 135 S Ct 2507, 2513; 576 US 519, 524; 192 L Ed 2d 514 (2015)

Disability Discrimination

The amendment to the Fair Housing Act prohibits discrimination against any person in the terms, conditions, or privileges of a dwelling, or in the provision of services or facilities in connection with a dwelling, because they are disabled. In some instances, a community association will also be subject to the Americans with Disabilities Act; however, the Americans with Disabilities Act does not apply to most residential community associations because it only applies to places of public accommodation that the general public has the ability to access.

In order to demonstrate a violation of the Fair Housing Act based on a disability, a plaintiff must prove all of the following elements:

• The owner suffers from a disability.

• The owner requested a reasonable accommodation or modification to the rules, policies, practices, or services related to the use or enjoyment of a dwelling.

- The association refused the accommodation or modification.

- The association knew, or should have known, of the disability at the time of the refusal.

One of the most common disability-related issues under the Fair Housing Act is a request by an occupant to make a modification to a unit or common elements that would not otherwise be permitted under the governing documents. Whether an accommodation or modification based on a disability is warranted depends on whether the accommodation or modification would provide the disabled individual with an equal opportunity to use the dwelling, whether the accommodation or modification is necessary, and whether the accommodation or modification is reasonable. Accordingly, a community association must weigh these factors in determining whether to grant a requested accommodation or modification or whether a reasonable alternative exists that could be offered to the person requesting an accommodation or modification. It is important to remember that the Fair Housing Act only requires a community association to offer a "reasonable accommodation," not an "absolute accommodation."

The Michigan Condominium Act, specifically MCL 559.147a, also contains special rules related to disability-related requests that may result in noncompliance with the governing documents. Specifically, Michigan law allows an improvement or modification to facilitate access to or movement within the unit for persons with disabilities who reside in or regularly visit the unit or to alleviate conditions that could be hazardous to persons with disabilities who reside in or regularly visit the unit if a condominium association fails to respond to the request within 60 days. Accordingly, both state and federal law may require a deviation from the governing documents for disability-related reasons.

In addition to requests to modify a unit or the common elements, requests for emotional support animals for disability-related reasons have greatly increased in recent years. In 2020, HUD issued new guidance on what must be considered when determining whether an accommodation request related to an emotional support animal should be granted. Based on HUD guidance, community associations should be aware of the following:

- An association is not allowed to inquire about a disability that is readily observable. Blindness, deafness, mobility limitations, certain intellectual impairments, and neurological impairments are identified as being readily observable.

- Letters from a health care provider that were issued online and not by someone with personal knowledge of the requestor's disability are insufficient to establish the need for a reasonable accommodation without further documentation.

- HUD recommends that a supporting letter for an accommodation request identify the patient's name, whether the health care professional has a professional relationship with the requestor, the type of animal requested, whether the patient has a physical or mental impairment, whether the impairment substantially limits a major life activity or major bodily function, and whether the patient needs the animal for physical or emotional reasons.

- HUD states that a housing provider may ask whether the type of assistance or emotional support animal being requested is commonly kept in a household. The FHEO-2020-01 notice states that "a dog, cat, small bird, rabbit, hamster, gerbil, other rodent, fish, turtle, or other small, domesticated animal that is traditionally kept in the home for pleasure rather than for commercial purposes" are animals that would typically qualify for a reasonable accommodation that would not substantially interfere with the operations of a condominium or homeowners association. On the other hand, HUD states that "reptiles (other than turtles), barnyard animals, monkeys, kangaroos, and other non-domesticated animals are not considered common household animals." The <u>FHEO-2020-01 notice</u> indicates that a requestor would have a substantial burden to meet in demonstrating that a non-household animal is necessary to accommodate a disability.

- HUD recommends that an association decide to accommodate a request for an emotional support animal within 10 days of receiving a request.

In some instances, it is possible that a community association will be faced with <u>competing requests</u> for reasonable accommodations that conflict. By way of example, a case in Iowa required a court to evaluate whether to permit an emotional support dog when another occupant of the building had severe allergies to pet dander. The court ultimately held that the request for an emotional support dog did not need to be granted because the request posed a direct threat to the other occupant of the building, the other occupant moved in first in reliance on the no-pets policy, and the requestor of the emotional support animal could have brought up the request before they moved in, as opposed to after.

Familial Discrimination

Familial discrimination claims are another common issue that community associations may encounter. Examples of people that are protected based on familial status include:

- Families with children under the age of 18.

- Pregnant persons.

- Any person in the process of securing legal custody of a minor child, including adoptive or foster parents.

- Persons with written permission of a parent or legal guardian.

In the context of community associations, familial discrimination claims most often arise from issues related to the use of common elements by <u>minors</u> and treating families with minors differently than owners in adult-only households. Many associations may not see an issue with rules regarding the use of pools and other common elements by unsupervised children or requiring children to be supervised at certain hours; however, on more than one occasion, <u>subjective rules</u> regarding children and teens have been found to violate the Fair Housing Act. Examples of rules where courts have found violations of the Fair Housing Act based on familial discrimination are as follows:

- **"All persons under the age of 18 must be in their home or back patio after sunset"** and **"There will be no loitering—congregating on the streets of [the development] [—] at any time. After dark all children should be in their home or on their patio."** *Fair Hous Ctr of the Greater Palm Beaches, Inc v Sonoma Bay Community Homeowners Ass'n, Inc*, 682 Fed App'x 768 (CA 11, 2017). The association justified these rules based on safety concerns and crime prevention; however, the court rejected these arguments because the association did not provide evidence that children had a propensity to commit criminal acts or that the children's parents could not supervise their outdoor activities at night.

- **"Children on the premises are to be supervised by a responsible adult at all times,"** **"Children under the age of 18 are not allowed in the pool or pool area at any time unless accompanied by their parents or legal guardian,"** and **"When the building lights come on all children are to be in their apartments."** <u>*Iniestra v Cliff Warren Investments, 886 F Supp 2d 1161 (CD Cal, 2012)*</u>. The apartment complex justified these rules based on concerns that children would play around the mechanical gate that permitted vehicles to enter and exit the complex and because there was no lifeguard on duty at the pool. The court rejected these arguments, explaining that the adult supervision rule throughout the entire premises was broader than the purpose of keeping children safe near the mechanical gate and that the adult supervision rule for the swimming pool was not an efficient method of promoting pool safety, particularly because it was possible for younger children to be better swimmers than older adults.

• **"All children 10 and under must be supervised by an Adult while outside," "Persons under the age of 18 must abide by the set curfew of 10:00 P.M.," "Children under the age of 14 years old must be accompanied by their parent or legal guardian at all times," "No persons under the age of 18 will be allowed to use the facility under any circumstances without ADULT RESIDENT supervision," and "No one under the age of 12 is allowed to use the Pool Table under any circumstances at any time."** _Pack v Fort Washington II_, 689 F Supp 2d 1237 (ED Cal, 2009). The apartment complex justified these rules based on safety concerns and the residents' ability to enjoy the premises. The court held that the adult supervision rule for all children 10 and under was overbroad because it would prohibit a child from reading outside just a few steps away from the apartment. For the remaining rules, the court held that they impermissibly contained a statement that indicates a preference for or limitation on families with children.

• **"Children will not be allowed to play or run around inside the building area at any time because of disturbance to other tenants or damage to building property."** _Fair Hous Congress v Weber_, 993 F Supp 1286 (CD Cal, 1997). The apartment complex justified this rule based on safety concerns for the children and maintaining quiet in the community. The court disregarded these arguments, explaining that the rule was so overbroad that it prohibited all children's play, including a "quiet, safe game of checkers."

- "During the summer season when the pool is open, the Recreation Center Manager will unlock the Clubhouse for ADULT USE ONLY," "No member or guest under the age of 14 may use the pool or spa unless accompanied by an adult (19 or older) member or adult guardian authorized by an adult member," "Guests are limited to six (6) per household. Residents 14 through 18 years of age are limited to one guest per person notwithstanding the household limit," "Adults have court privileges over children after 3:00 p.m. weekdays and any time on weekends or holidays," and "Quiet Swimming Only in Pool & Jacuzzi." *Hill v River Run Homeowners Ass'n, Inc*, 438 F Supp 3d 1155, 1173-74 (D Idaho, 2020). The association justified these rules based on concerns related to damage and vandalism, overcrowding, and possible criminal activity by teenagers. The court rejected these arguments, explaining that the rules were overbroad and that adults can also overcrowd and vandalize the pool and surrounding area, yet they were allowed up to six guests.

As Fair Housing Act violations can incur significant financial penalties, it is wise to consult with legal counsel before implementing or attempting to enforce rules that may adversely impact families. As demonstrated by the above examples, many rules that discriminate against families may be well intentioned but end up creating significant issues.

The Fair Housing Act, though, specifically the portion known as the Housing for Older Persons Act ("HOPA"), does provide one exception in which discrimination is permitted based on familial status. HOPA permits 55+ condominiums to be formed, without violating the Fair Housing Act, if the following requirements are satisfied:

- 80% of the condominium's units are occupied by at least one person who is 55 years of age or older.

- The condominium must be marketed as a 55+ community and the condominium documents, rules, and policies must reflect that the condominium is a 55+ community.

After qualifying as a HOPA community, the condominium association is required to perform a survey at least every two years to ensure that the age and occupancy requirements in the governing documents are satisfied.

Race, Color, or National Origin Discrimination

The Fair Housing Act also prohibits community associations from discriminating based on race, color, or national origin. Fortunately, most associations can avoid overt race, color, or national origin discrimination claims simply by exercising common sense and not taking actions based on these types of protected classes. Most modern community association documents do not contain provisions that would discriminate based on race, color, or national origin. Unfortunately, though, many older declarations may contain language that limits sales or occupation to members of a certain race or ethnicity. Associations should be aware that republishing these governing documents, even if the discriminatory provisions are not enforced, may result in a discrimination claim. Specifically, 42 USC 3604(c) of the Fair Housing Act makes the following unlawful:

> To make, print, or publish, or cause to be made, printed, or published any notice, statement, or advertisement, with respect to the sale or rental of a dwelling that indicates any preference, limitation, or discrimination based on race, color, religion, sex, handicap, familial status, or national origin, or an intention to make any such preference, limitation, or discrimination.

Accordingly, continuing to republish discriminatory provisions which have never been removed from community association documents could inadvertently lead to a fair housing claim. Fortunately, the Michigan legislature passed <u>HB 4416</u> at the end of 2022, which provides a simple procedure for condominium and homeowner association boards to remove discriminatory provisions from governing documents without holding a vote of all the owners.

Finally, community associations should also be aware that even if the association itself is not engaging in discrimination, in certain circumstances the Fair Housing Act may require a community association to intervene in neighbor-to-neighbor discrimination. Specifically, a community association can violate the Fair Housing Act by creating a <u>hostile environment</u>. The regulations to the Fair Housing Act, 24 CFR § 100.7(a)(1)(iii), state that "A person is directly liable for ... [f]ailing to take prompt action to correct and end a discriminatory housing practice by a third-party, where the person knew or should have known of the discriminatory conduct and had the power to correct it."

Associations should be aware that at least one court has determined that a plaintiff sufficiently alleged a Fair Housing Act violation based on a <u>hostile environment theory</u> when the association enforced the provisions of the governing documents against an owner that did not pay assessments but took no action to enforce the provisions of the governing documents when the same owner engaged in egregious racially discriminatory conduct against another owner. Accordingly, community associations should be aware not only that direct discrimination based on race, color, or national origin is a violation of the Fair Housing Act, but a violation can also be established based on a failure to intervene when one occupant is discriminating against another occupant in the association.

Religious Discrimination

A Fair Housing Act violation may be established if a community association adopts a policy that intentionally discriminates against a particular religion or adopts a policy that has a disparate impact against a particular religion. Specifically, to establish a religious discrimination claim, a plaintiff must demonstrate that a <u>discriminatory purpose</u> was a motivating factor behind the association's actions or that the actions of the association had a <u>disparate impact</u> on owners that held certain religious beliefs. A disparate impact claim may be established by demonstrating that the decision of the community association had a segregative effect or that it made housing options significantly more restrictive for members of a particular religion than for persons outside that religion. Community associations should also be aware that the "reasonable accommodation" language that applies to disability-related requests under the Fair Housing Act is not applicable to religious issues. Accordingly, a community association does not have to grant a "reasonable accommodation" for religious purposes as long as all religions are treated equally.

Religious discrimination claims may arise in the context of determining whether to permit religious services within the community. <u>Religious discrimination claims can be avoided</u> if a community association treats all religions the same. Accordingly, it is acceptable to completely ban religious ceremonies if the ban applies equally to all religious denominations. Problems may arise, though, when an association adopts policies that provide a preference to one religion over another. By way of example, if an association were to allow one religious group to hold a service, but not allow another religious group to hold a service or impose additional burdens on a certain type of religious group, it is possible that a Fair Housing Act violation could occur.

In the context of holding religious services within a home or condominium unit, other courts have also held that a community association may enforce facially neutral restrictive covenants when religious ceremonies violate the restrictive covenants. Specifically, a Texas court held that a community association could <u>abate a nuisance</u> when a home was primarily being used for religious worship, as opposed to residential use, and the religious services were not merely incidental to a residential use of the property. Accordingly, while owners are generally permitted to privately worship within the confines of their home or unit, if they change the exterior appearance, create traffic issues, or otherwise violate the restrictive covenants, the association may still be able to prevent religious services that interfere with the rights of other owners.

Another religious discrimination issue that may arise from time to time involves the display of religious symbols. Generally, federal courts have held that the governing documents can broadly prohibit exterior decorations in a community association. By way of example, one federal court ruled that an owner was required to take down a Jhandee, a Hindu religious symbol, that was displayed in violation of the condominium bylaws. The court determined that the condominium association uniformly enforced the restrictions and the association did not have a discriminatory purpose for enforcing the facially neutral restrictions so no violation of the Fair Housing Act occurred. In contrast, another federal court held that a factual issue existed as to whether the Fair Housing Act had been violated when a condominium association attempted to take enforcement action to have a mezuzah, a Jewish religious symbol, removed from the common areas. While the condominium association's rules related to items in the hallway were facially neutral, the court found that the association permitted other non-religious items to remain in the hallway, in violation of its policy, and that derogatory comments may have been made by the association about the Jewish faith. Accordingly, consistent enforcement of restrictive covenants is important to avoid potential religious discrimination claims.

Finally, one other common issue that community associations encounter related to religion involves holiday displays. Once again, the key to regulating holiday displays is to create and enforce uniform rules when it comes to issues related to the time, location, and size of a holiday display. As one state court noted, "massive commercial lighting displays generated by commercial transformers are not appropriate in quiet residential neighborhoods" and may violate the restrictive covenants without running afoul of the Fair Housing Act; however, it is worth noting that a homeowner in Idaho obtained a $75,000 judgment from a jury for a violation of the Fair Housing Act based on a claim that the homeowners association discriminated against his Christian beliefs in attempting to require him to remove his extravagant Christmas display. Later, a federal court judge reversed the decision of the jury and found that the homeowners association did not violate the Fair Housing Act and the owner violated the restrictive covenants because:

- Section 5.4.1 of the covenants barred the use of a dwelling "for any purpose other than a single-family residential purpose." The owner's stated purpose for hosting the Christmas program was to raise money for charities and engage in ministry. Furthermore, the owner decorated their home in 2015 and 2016 with hundreds of thousands of lights and attracted thousands of people to attend and take part in the Christmas program. The homeowners association showed by a preponderance of the evidence that the owner in 2015 and 2016 used their home for purposes other than "single-family residential" use.

- Section 5.4.2 of the covenants "prohibit[s] ... any activity which would in any way interfere with the quiet enjoyment of any [other] Owner." The owner's Christmas program interfered with the ability of other homeowners to quietly enjoy their own homes in a number of ways: (1) the owner used speakers outside of the home to amplify sound, (2) the busses employed by the owner blocked traffic and created noise, (3) the cars parked by non-residents blocked traffic, (4) the thousands of people who attended the Christmas program created excessive congestion in the neighborhood and temporarily changed and destroyed the quiet, suburban nature and appearance of the subdivision.

- Section 5.4.3 of the covenants prohibits "sign[s] of any kind ... [from being] displayed to the public ... without prior written committee approval." Part of the advertising for the owner's Christmas program included the placement of a large sign on their front lawn.

- Section 5.4.9 of the covenants prohibits "activities ... conducted on the Property ... which are or *might be unsafe* or hazardous to any person or property." The owner's Christmas program generated significant traffic and parking issues. Given the congestion, emergency personnel responding to an incident would have difficulty accessing certain houses close to the owner's home.

- Section 5.5.2 of the covenants states "No reptiles, livestock, poultry, or birds of any kind shall be raised, bred or kept on any lot, or any portion of this property." The owner kept both a camel and donkey on their property as part of their recreation of the Nativity Scene. Both animals fell within the category of livestock.

- Section 11.5.2 of the covenants states "failure of any Owner of a Lot to comply with any provision ... [of the Declaration] is ... a nuisance." The owner's Christmas program violated Sections 5.1.3, 5.4.1, 5.4.2, 5.4.3, 5.4.9, 5.4.15, and 5.5.2. Accordingly, the homeowners association showed by a preponderance of the evidence that the owner's Christmas program was a nuisance that violated Section 11.5.2 of the Declaration.

Morris v W Hayden Estates First Addition Homeowners Ass'n, Inc, 382 F Supp 3d 1093, 1111–13 (D Idaho, 2019). While the trial court's decision is on appeal, the decision is instructive as to what types of facially neutral covenants a homeowners association may uniformly enforce in regulating holiday decorations without running afoul of the Fair Housing Act.

While religious discrimination is generally prohibited, the Fair Housing Act does contain a limited exception for certain religious organizations. Specifically, 42 USC 3607 provides, in pertinent part:

> Nothing in this subchapter shall prohibit a religious organization, association, or society, or any nonprofit institution or organization operated, supervised or controlled by or in conjunction with a religious organization, association, or society, from limiting the sale, rental or occupancy of dwellings which it owns or operates for other than a commercial purpose to persons of the same religion, or from giving preference to such persons, unless membership in such religion is restricted on account of race, color, or national origin.

In order to qualify for an exemption, a community association would need to demonstrate that it is: (1) a religious organization or (2) a non-profit organization "operated, supervised or controlled by or in conjunction with" a religious organization. Whether a community association can qualify under either of these standards is highly fact-specific, and in most cases, courts have held that community associations that are only loosely affiliated with a specific religion are not entitled to the above exemption.

Sex Discrimination

The Fair Housing Act also protects occupants against discrimination based on sex. Specifically, 42 USC § 3604(b) of the Fair Housing Act prohibits discrimination "in the terms, conditions, or privileges of sale or rental of a dwelling, or in the provision of services or facilities in connection therewith" because of a person's sex. 42 USC § 3617 of the Fair Housing Act also makes it unlawful to "coerce, intimidate, threaten, or interfere with any person in the enjoyment" of their rights under the Fair Housing Act. Accordingly, common sense would dictate that any form of sexual harassment, such as unwanted advancement, inappropriate comments, or offers of quid pro quo for sexual favors, would violate the Fair Housing Act.

Similarly, as discussed above in the context of racial discrimination, a community association may be exposed to liability if they do not take action to prevent sex discrimination based on a hostile environment theory. HUD has implemented rules, specifically 24 CFR § 100.600(a)(2), that define a hostile environment as follows:

> … unwelcome conduct that is sufficiently severe or pervasive as to interfere with: The availability, sale, rental, or use or enjoyment of a dwelling; the terms, conditions, or privileges of the sale or rental, or the provision or enjoyment of services or facilities in connection therewith; or the availability, terms, or conditions of a residential real estate-related transaction. Hostile environment harassment does not require a change in the economic benefits, terms, or conditions of the dwelling or housing-related services or facilities, or of the residential real-estate transaction.

HUD also standardized how to determine if the unwelcome conduct rises to the level of hostile environment harassment. 24 CFR § 100.600(a)(2)(i) states that "whether hostile environment harassment exists depends upon the totality of the circumstances," listing the following considerations:

- Factors to be considered to determine whether hostile environment harassment exists include, but are not limited to, the nature of the conduct, the context in which the incident(s) occurred, the severity, scope, frequency, duration, and location of the conduct, and the relationships of the persons involved.

- Neither psychological nor physical harm must be demonstrated to prove that a hostile environment exists. Evidence of psychological or physical harm may, however, be relevant in determining whether a hostile environment existed and, if so, the amount of damages to which an aggrieved person may be entitled.

- Whether unwelcome conduct is sufficiently severe or pervasive as to create a hostile environment is evaluated from the perspective of a reasonable person in the aggrieved person's position.

In addition to sexual harassment, sex discrimination may also include the implementation of rules or policies by a community association that provide preference to one sex over another. By way of example, a federal court held that a pool policy that had separate times for men and women to swim violated the Fair Housing Act:

Looking to the express terms of the pool policy, the Association emphasizes that it allows for roughly equal swimming time for both men and women in the aggregate. But this is not enough to save the pool schedule, which discriminates in its allotment of different times to men and women in addition to employing sex as its criterion. Under the most recent version of the schedule, women are able to swim for only 3.5 hours after 5:00 p.m. on weeknights, compared to 16.5 hours for men. The schedule also assigns to men the entire period from 4:00 p.m. onward on Friday afternoons. Women with regular-hour jobs thus have little access to the pool during the work week, and the schedule appears to reflect particular assumptions about the roles of men and women.... In light of these specific inequitable features, the schedule discriminates against women under the FHA even though it provides roughly equal aggregate swimming time to each gender.

Curto v A Country Place Condo Ass'n, Inc, 921 F3d 405, 410–11 (CA 3, 2019).

Finally, community associations should be aware that HUD has also indicated that discrimination based on <u>gender identity and sexual orientation</u> will also be treated as form of sex discrimination. Accordingly, community associations should not implement policies that would discriminate based on gender identity or sexual orientation.

Conclusion

Your Condo or HOA Is What You Make of It!

As you have reached the end of Hirzel's Handbook, you should understand the basic principles that you need to run a community association. By now, you should have a good grasp on the following:

- Understanding the different types of community associations

- Best practices for operating a condominium or homeowners association

- Navigating the developer turnover process

- Enforcing the governing documents

- Collecting delinquent assessments

- Knowing when to amend the governing documents

- Complying with the Fair Housing Act

While this book and the linked articles have provided a lot of important information, it is now up to you to implement the best practices outlined above in order to successfully operate your community association! Just remember, a community association is only as good as the people running it!

It is inevitable that there will be bumps in the road. Some community associations will have more problems than others. If you are concerned at all about a dispute with an owner, the clarity of some of your governing documents, or any other issues regarding the operation and maintenance of your community, please do not hesitate to reach out to me. I love talking with board members and the initial consultation for a community association is always free. You can reach me by calling (248) 478-1800, emailing me at kevin@hirzel-law.com, or by filling out our online contact form.

I also would appreciate any feedback you would like to send me on the book. I do my best to translate legal terminology into an easy-to-understand format, but if something is unclear, your feedback may help me further clarify that issue for future readers. Also, if you think there are any topics that I have missed, I would like to know that, too. Finally, if you found the book helpful, I would greatly appreciate a review on Amazon. For Kindle readers, please continue to the next page and rate this book.

What To Do Next

Did you find Hirzel's Handbook helpful? Please leave a positive review here

Index

T

Taxes, 8, 106, 107
Transitional control date, 59, 61, 72
Types of condominium, 1, 2, 4

V

Voting, 6, 24, 25, 28, 68, 114, 124

W

Wi-Fi, 121

Appendix A

Operations Checklist

- File Annual Reports with LARA

    o   Almost all condominium and homeowners associations in Michigan are nonprofit corporations. Pursuant to <u>MCL 450.2911</u>, nonprofit corporations are required to <u>file annual reports</u> with the Department of Licensing and Regulatory Affairs ("LARA") by October 1st each year.

- Hold Annual Meetings

    o   Pursuant to <u>MCL 450.2402</u>, condominium and homeowners associations that are nonprofit corporations must hold an annual membership meeting; however, in some cases, the meeting can be held completely online or at a polling location. A board also has discretion on whether to permit the membership to attend its regular board meetings.

- Take Meeting Minutes

  o The <u>Michigan Nonprofit Corporation Act</u> indicates that associations should take meeting minutes for board, committee, and membership meetings. Associations should take minutes to have a historical record of the decisions that were made at each meeting for future boards to rely on.

- Create an Annual Budget and Analyze Reserve Funds

  o Almost all governing documents require an association to create an annual budget that is used to calculate assessments. It is helpful to have a reserve study performed every three years as part of the budgeting process to determine if the association's reserves are adequate as well.

- Prepare Financial Statements

  o Almost all condominium and homeowners associations are required to produce annual financial statements. In many cases, the governing documents require that the financial statement be audited or reviewed by an accountant. <u>MCL 559.157</u> of the <u>Michigan Condominium Act</u> requires condominium associations to have an audit or review performed on an annual basis if they have revenue in excess of $20,000, unless the membership votes to opt out of the audit or review.

- File Annual Tax Returns with the State and Federal Governments

  o Condominium and homeowners associations must file state and federal tax returns on an annual basis. The specific required <u>forms</u> and timing can depend on the structure and sources of income so be sure to check with an accountant to make sure you are on track.

- Enforce the Bylaws

  o One of the primary jobs of a condominium or home-owners association is to <u>enforce the restrictive covenants as written</u>. We recommend that every association have a bylaw enforcement policy in place to ensure that the governing documents are uniformly enforced. Examples of common bylaw enforcement actions include aesthetic issues, illegal activity, landscaping, noise, pets, parking, smoking, or unauthorized modifications of common areas or homes. Many governing documents permit an association to recover attorney's fees and costs if the association is forced to take an owner to court.

- Know the Exceptions Related to Bylaw Enforcement

  o In some cases, the governing documents provide discretion to a board to deviate from enforcing the documents. While this is somewhat uncommon, there are times that federal or state law requires an association to make an exception to normal bylaw enforcement procedures for reasons related to disability, familial status, race, color, religion, sex, or national origin. An attorney should always be consulted if the board has questions about whether there are exceptions to enforcing the bylaws.

- Collect Assessments from Delinquent Co-owners

  o Assessments are collected on a monthly, quarterly, or annual basis, depending on the requirements of the governing documents. We recommend that every association have a <u>collection policy</u> in place to ensure that the association's cash flow is not interrupted and that all delinquent owners go through the same process. If an owner fails to pay assessments, most governing documents will permit an association to place a lien, foreclose on that lien, and recover attorney's fees and costs if the owner ultimately fails to make suitable payment arrangements.

- Amend Outdated Governing Documents

    o Community associations should regularly review their governing documents to ensure smooth operations and avoid exposure to litigation. Signs that the governing documents may need to be amended include: (1) the governing documents have not been updated to account for the 2015 and 2018 amendments to the <u>Michigan Nonprofit Corporation Act</u>, (2) the governing documents were not updated after developer turnover, (3) the governing documents do not address technological or societal changes related to cameras, drones, electric vehicles, short-term rentals, social media, smartphone use, smoking, or solar panels, and (4) the governing documents are unclear or conflict with each other. Hirzel Law offers Condo and HOA report cards so associations can determine whether their governing documents need to be amended to address these issues.

Appendix B

Community Association Loan Checklist

- Name, address, and number of units in the community association
- Board or association meeting minutes in which the loan was authorized
- Financial statements for the community association from the last 2 years
- The most recent tax return for the community association
- The current budget and year-to-date financials
- The current delinquency report that demonstrates the number of co-owners that were 60+ days delinquent during the past 6-9 months

- A list of owners and tenants to determine the owner-occupancy rate

- The association's governing documents

A reserve study or engineering report that describes the condition of the building or common elements

- Contact information for the association's attorney, accountant, insurance agent, management company (if any), and board members

- Dollar amount requested, detailed description of project and cost estimates, copies of bids, and executed contracts that the money would be used for

Appendix C

---✠---

Fannie Mae Guidelines

The Fannie Mae lending guidelines indicate that the following types of condominiums will be ineligible for financing:

Loans secured by units in a condominium with significant deferred maintenance or that have received a directive from a regulatory authority or inspection agency to make repairs due to unsafe conditions will no longer be eligible for purchase by Fannie Mae. Significant deferred maintenance is defined as any one of the following:

- Full or partial evacuation of the condominium or co-op to complete repairs is required for more than seven days or an unknown period of time.

- The condominium or co-op has deficiencies, defects, substantial damage, or deferred maintenance that is one of the following:

1. Severe enough to affect the safety, soundness, structural integrity, or habitability of the improvements.

2. The improvements need substantial repairs and rehabilitation, including many major components.

3. Impedes the safe and sound functioning of one or more of the condominium's or co-op's major structural or mechanical elements, including, but not limited to, the foundation, roof, load bearing structures, electrical system, HVAC, or plumbing.

Conditions in Condos that Will Not Impact Fannie Mae Lending

In Fannie Mae Lender Letter (LL-2021-14), Fannie Mae clarified that not every defect in a condominium will prevent a potential purchaser from obtaining a loan. Specifically, the following types of issues will not make a condominium project ineligible:

- Routine maintenance or repairs that a homeowners association undertakes to maintain or preserve the integrity and condition of its property.

- Damage or deferred maintenance that is isolated to one or a few units that does not affect the overall safety, soundness, structural integrity, or habitability of the improvements.

Freddie Mac

Repairs and replacements that significantly impact the safety, soundness, structural integrity, or habitability of the project's building(s) and/or that impact unit values, financial viability, or marketability of the project. These repairs and replacements include:

- All life safety hazards

- Violations of any federal, state, or local law, ordinance, or code relating to zoning, subdivision and use, building, housing accessibility, health matters, or fire safety

- Material deficiencies

- Significant deferred maintenance

Conditions in Condos that Will Not Impact Freddie Mac Lending

Similar to the Fannie Mae guidelines, Freddie Mac clarified that not every defect in a condominium will prevent a potential purchaser from obtaining a loan. Specifically, the following types of issues will not make a condominium project ineligible under the Freddie Mac Guidelines for routine repairs and maintenance, which is defined as follows:

Repairs and maintenance that are expected to be completed by the project in the normal course of business and are nominal in cost. These repairs are not considered to be critical and include work that is:

- Often preventative in nature

- Accomplished within the project's normal operating budget

- Typically completed by on-site staff

- Focused on keeping the project fully functioning and serviceable

- Minor deficiencies with a cost of $3,000 or less per repair item that do not warrant immediate attention but that require repairs or replacements that should be undertaken within the next 12 months

- Scheduled repairs and maintenance that are fully funded, may have a cost greater than $3,000, and will be undertaken within the next 12 months

Damage or deferred maintenance to one or a few units in the project, provided that there is no impact to the overall safety, soundness, structural integrity, or habitability of the improvements

Made in the USA
Columbia, SC
31 March 2023

14551423R00109